I0429216

Water Use, Availability, and Net Demand in the Tennessee River Watershed within Alabama, 2005

By Amy C. Gill, Michael J. Harper, and Thomas M. Littlepage

Prepared in cooperation with the Alabama Department of Economic and Community Affairs, Office of Water Resources

Scientific Investigations Report 2013–5067

U.S. Department of the Interior
U.S. Geological Survey

U.S. Department of the Interior
SALLY JEWELL, Secretary

U.S. Geological Survey
Suzette M. Kimball, Acting Director

U.S. Geological Survey, Reston, Virginia: 2013

For more information on the USGS—the Federal source for science about the Earth, its natural and living resources, natural hazards, and the environment, visit http://www.usgs.gov or call 1–888–ASK–USGS.

For an overview of USGS information products, including maps, imagery, and publications, visit http://www.usgs.gov/pubprod

To order this and other USGS information products, visit http://store.usgs.gov

Suggested citation:
Gill, A.C., Harper, M.J., and Littlepage, T.M., 2013, Water use, availability, and net demand in the Tennessee River watershed within Alabama, 2005: U.S. Geological Survey Scientific Investigations Report 2013–5067, 42 p.

Contents

Figures

Tables

Conversion Factors and Datums

Multiply	By	To obtain
Length		
inch	2.54	centimeter (cm)
inch	25.4	millimeter (mm)
foot (ft)	0.3048	meter (m)
mile (mi)	1.609	kilometer (km)
Area		
acre	4,047	square meter (m^2)
square mile (mi^2)	259.0	hectare (ha)
square mile (mi^2)	2.590	square kilometer (km^2)
Volume		
gallon (gal)	3.785	liter (L)
gallon (gal)	0.003785	cubic meter (m^3)
gallon (gal)	3.785	cubic decimeter (dm^3)
million gallons (Mgal)	3,785	cubic meter (m^3)
acre-foot (acre-ft)	1,233	cubic meter (m^3)
Flow rate		
acre-foot per day (acre-ft/d)	0.01427	cubic meter per second (m^3/s)
acre-foot per year (acre-ft/yr)	1,233	cubic meter per year (m^3/yr)
gallon per day (gal/d)	0.003785	cubic meter per day (m^3/d)
million gallons per day (Mgal/d)	0.04381	cubic meter per second (m^3/s)
inch per year (in/yr)	25.4	millimeter per year (mm/yr)
cubic foot per second (ft^3/s)	0.02832	cubic meter per second (m^3/s)
Energy		
kilowatt-hour (kWh)	3,600,000	joule (J)
Application rate		
gallon per day per acre	0.003785	cubic meter per day per acre
gallon per day per square mile [(gal/d)/mi^2]	0.001461	cubic meter per day per square kilometer [(m^3/s)/km^2]
cubic foot per second per square mile [(ft^3/s)/mi^2]	0.01093	cubic meter per second per square kilometer [(m^3/s)/km^2]

Temperature in degrees Celsius (°C) may be converted to degrees Fahrenheit (°F) as follows:

°F = (1.8 × °C) + 32

Temperature in degrees Fahrenheit (°F) may be converted to degrees Celsius (°C) as follows:

°C = (°F – 32) / 1.8

Horizontal coordinate information is referenced to North American Datum of 1983 (NAD 83).

Acronyms and Abbreviations Used in this Report

ADAI	Alabama Department of Agriculture and Industries
ADECA	Alabama Department of Economic and Community Affairs
ADEM	Alabama Department of Environmental Management
ARWA	Alabama Rural Water Association
AWURP	Alabama Water Use Reporting Program
CP	county population
DOE–EIA	U.S. Department of Energy, Energy Information Administration
DWB–ADEM	Drinking Water Branch, Alabama Department of Environmental Management
GIS	geographic information system
GSA	Geological Survey of Alabama
HH	housing unit
HH-PS	number of housing units on public supply
HUC	hydrologic unit code
MOR	monthly operating report
NASS	National Agricultural Statistics Service (USDA)
NWUIP	National Water-Use Information Program (USGS)
OWR	Office of Water Resources (Alabama)
PCTHH-PS	percent of housing units on public supply
P-HH	persons per housing unit
PP-PS	population served by public supply
SDWIS	Safe Drinking Water Information System (USEPA)
SIC	Standard Industrial Classification
TVA	Tennessee Valley Authority
USDA	U.S. Department of Agriculture
USGS	U.S. Geological Survey
USEPA	U.S. Environmental Protection Agency

Water Use, Availability, and Net Demand in the Tennessee River Watershed within Alabama, 2005

By Amy C. Gill, Michael J. Harper, and Thomas M. Littlepage

Abstract

The U.S. Geological Survey worked in cooperation with the Alabama Department of Economic and Community Affairs–Office of Water Resources to estimate water use and water availability for 2005 for the portion of the Tennessee River watershed contained within the borders of the State of Alabama. Estimates of water use and availability are an important part of planning for population and economic growth in the Tennessee River watershed in Alabama. Total water use for the region in 2005 was 5,197 million gallons per day (Mgal/d). Total surface-water withdrawals were 5,139 Mgal/d, and total groundwater withdrawals were about 58 Mgal/d. About 92 percent of the total water withdrawn was surface water used for once-through cooling for thermoelectric power generation. Self-supplied industrial and public-supply water uses accounted for the next greatest uses of water, constituting approximately 49 and 42 percent, respectively, of the total water use excluding thermoelectric power use.

Summaries of water use by county and subbasin indicated the areas of greatest water withdrawals and use within the Tennessee River watershed. Limestone (2,012 Mgal/d), Jackson (1,498 Mgal/d), and Colbert (1,363 Mgal/d) Counties were the counties with the greatest total water use in 2005 and had large amounts of water withdrawn for thermoelectric power generation. When water use from thermoelectric power generation was not considered, the counties with the greatest withdrawals were Morgan (124 Mgal/d), Madison (72 Mgal/d), Colbert (69 Mgal/d), and Lawrence (67 Mgal/d). The subbasin with the greatest total water use was Wheeler Lake (2,260 Mgal/d) in the Middle Tennessee–Elk subregion. Wheeler Lake subbasin also had the greatest public-supply, irrigation, industrial, mining, and thermoelectric withdrawals of any subbasin in the Tennessee River watershed within Alabama.

Total water availability for the Tennessee River watershed within Alabama was estimated to be 34,567 Mgal/d by the Geological Survey of Alabama. Net water demand for the watershed was calculated by subtracting the Tennessee Valley Authority estimates of return flow from water withdrawals. The net water demand was 136 Mgal/d, which is less than 1 percent of the estimated water available.

Introduction

The State of Alabama is expected to experience population growth and simultaneous increased water demand during the next 25 to 30 years (The University of Alabama, Center for Business and Economic Research, 2011). Planning for the increased demand on the State's finite water supply is crucial to ensure that adequate amounts of water are available for beneficial uses. Compilations of water use have been created every 5 years for the last 55 years in the State of Alabama (MacKichan, 1951, 1957; MacKichan and Kammerer, 1961; Murray, 1968; Murray and Reeves, 1972, 1977; Solley and others, 1983, 1988, 1993, 1998; Hutson and others, 2004a, 2009). These compilations provide a record of water use through time that can be used to assess trends within the State and to evaluate probable future demands. An important further step in planning for future water demand is to link current known water use to estimates of total water availability.

The Tennessee River watershed within Alabama is a high-priority area for future water-use planning for the State of Alabama because of high water withdrawal rates, the presence of large population centers, thermoelectric power generation, industry, and the Federal interest in the flow of the river. The Tennessee River watershed historically has been intensively used for water withdrawals (Hutson and others, 2004b). In 2005, thermoelectric power generation and industrial uses in the Tennessee River watershed within Alabama accounted for 58 and 39 percent, respectively, of statewide withdrawals for those categories of use. Population of the watershed was approximately 19 percent of the statewide population, and Huntsville and Decatur, the State's fourth and eighth largest cities, respectively, are located within the watershed. The Tennessee Valley Authority (TVA) manages flow and reservoir volume along the Tennessee River to achieve goals for hydroelectric power generation, navigation, flood damage reduction, and water supply.

Water managers within the State need water-use, availability, and net demand data to adequately plan for the multiple uses of the water resources within the Tennessee River watershed. To address this need, the Alabama Department of Economic and Community Affairs—Office of Water

Resources (ADECA-OWR) worked in cooperation with the U.S. Geological Survey (USGS) to estimate water use and availability for the watershed. For this report, data that were compiled as part of the statewide water use report in 2005 were supplemented by more detailed local data available for the Tennessee River watershed, including net demand data from the Tennessee Valley Authority and water availability estimates made by the Geological Survey of Alabama (GSA).

Purpose and Scope

This report summarizes current (2005) water use and groundwater and surface-water availability for the Tennessee River watershed into a format that can be used for initial water planning efforts. The USGS developed this summary in cooperation with the ADECA-OWR. The collection and reporting of water use and water availability information are a priority issue in the USGS Science Strategy (U.S. Geological Survey, 2007a). Water-use estimates are presented by source of supply, by water-use category, by county, and by hydrologic subregion and subbasin. Water-use information is presented as total water use and as water use for each of seven categories: public supply, residential, irrigation, livestock, industrial, mining, and thermoelectric power. Water availability estimates are provided by source of supply and hydrologic subregion and subbasin. In addition, net water demand in the Tennessee River watershed is discussed.

The Tennessee River watershed area of Alabama was chosen as a pilot for this type of watershed-based study because of the existence of previous investigations of water availability and the likelihood that the area will have substantial population growth in the coming decades (The University of Alabama, Center for Business and Economic Research, 2011). This initial assessment of water use, availability, and demand is intended to serve as a basis for designing more refined estimates in this watershed and other watersheds in the State of Alabama.

Hydrologic Setting

The Tennessee River enters northeastern Alabama from Tennessee and flows southwestward and then westward across Alabama before turning northwestward to exit the State at the northwestern corner and flow through Mississippi and Tennessee. The entire Tennessee River watershed drainage area is 40,910 square miles (mi^2) and includes parts of seven States. The Alabama portion of the watershed is 6,780 mi^2 or about 17 percent of the total watershed (Hutson and others,

2004b; fig. 1). The drainage area covers about 13 percent of the State of Alabama (Alabama Department of Conservation and Natural Resources, 2008) and includes all or part of 15 Alabama counties (fig. 2). Seven hydrologic subbasins of the Tennessee River watershed are completely or partially located within Alabama (fig. 3).

In Alabama, the Tennessee River is impounded by a series of dams operated by the TVA (fig. 4). On the mainstem of the Tennessee River, three dams, Guntersville, Wilson, and Wheeler, are located in Alabama, while a fourth dam, Pick-wick, located in Tennessee, forms a reservoir that is largely encompassed by the State of Alabama. In addition, TVA also operates four dams (Upper Bear Creek, Little Bear Creek, Cedar Creek, and Bear Creek Dams) in the watershed of Bear Creek, a northward-flowing tributary to the Tennessee River. TVA manages the dams and associated reservoirs to provide hydroelectric power generation, navigation, flood control, water supply, and recreation. The amount of water in the Tennessee River system and its reservoirs depends on rainfall and runoff (Tennessee Valley Authority, 2012). The Guntersville, Wheeler, Wilson, Pickwick, and Bear reservoir systems regulate flow in the Tennessee River system within Alabama.

Mean annual rainfall in the Alabama portion of the Tennessee River watershed is about 58 inches. For the period 1971–2000, the average annual rainfall at weather stations in the watershed ranged from a minimum of 53.56 to a maximum of 62.55 inches (National Oceanic and Atmospheric Administration, 2009). Monthly rainfall ranged from 2.96 to 6.84 inches during that period and generally is highest in March and lowest in August and October. Annual runoff, the amount of water discharged from an area in a year, either through overland flow or discharge to streams, for the same period (1971–2000) for the Tennessee River Valley was approximately 25.6 inches (U.S. Geological Survey, 2012). Runoff and streamflow are strongly associated with storm events because of the relatively impermeable rock underlying most of the watershed area.

Groundwater resources in the watershed are represented by three aquifer systems: the Southeastern Coastal Plain aquifer system, the Valley and Ridge aquifers, and the Appalachian Plateaus and Interior Low Plateaus aquifers (Miller, 1990; fig. 5). The Southeastern Coastal Plain aquifer system in Alabama consists mostly of sand and clay layers. The aquifer system crops out in the southwestern portion of the study area and includes the Tuscaloosa Group, an unconfined aquifer with low yields. The Tuscaloosa Group is productive enough to be used as a water supply by some small communities in the Tennessee River watershed (Bossong and Harris, 1987; Miller, 1990).

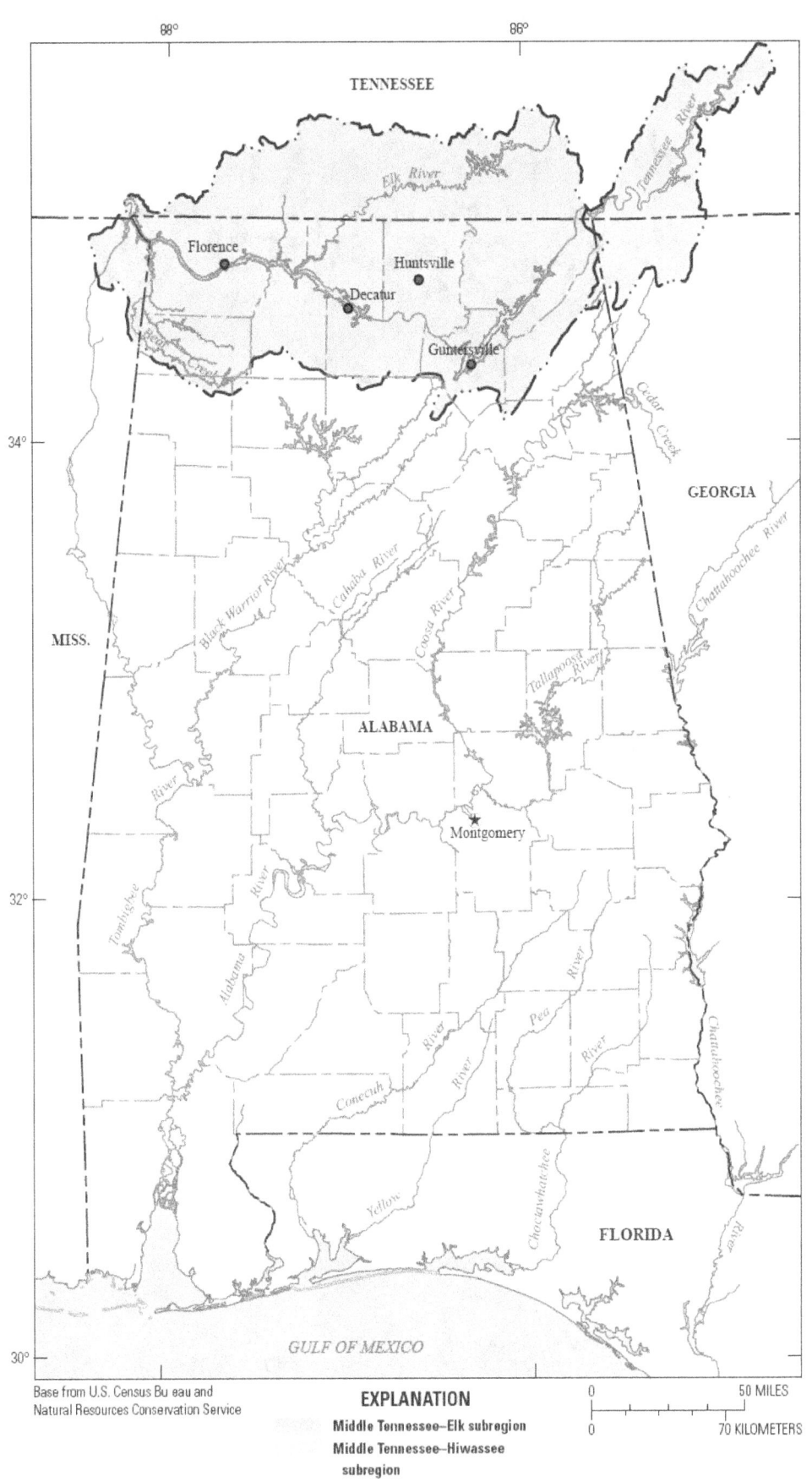

Figure 1. Hydrologic subregions, rivers, state capital, and study area cities in Alabama.

Base from U.S. Census Bureau and
Natural Resources Conservation Service

EXPLANATION

Middle Tennessee–Elk subregion

Middle Tennessee–Hiwassee
 subregion

·· ——— Subregion boundary

0   50 MILES

0   70 KILOMETERS

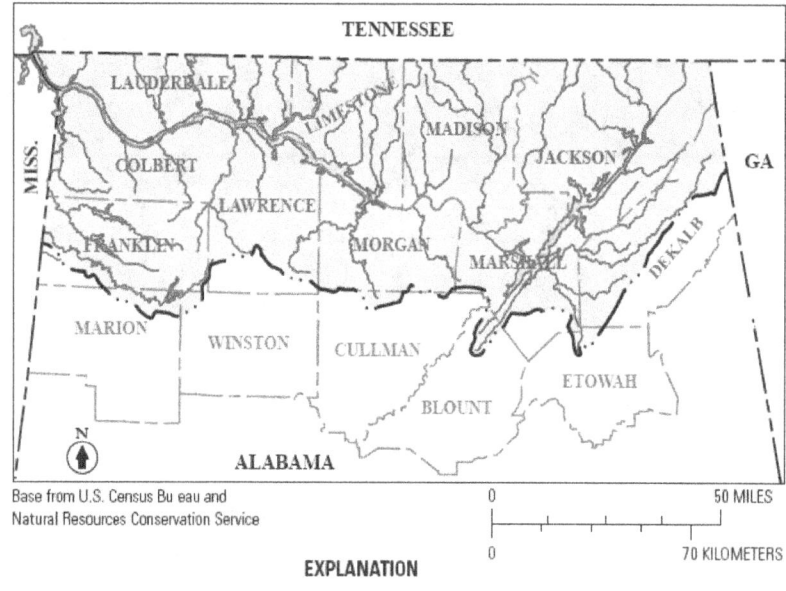

Figure 2. Alabama counties in and partially in the Tennessee River watershed.

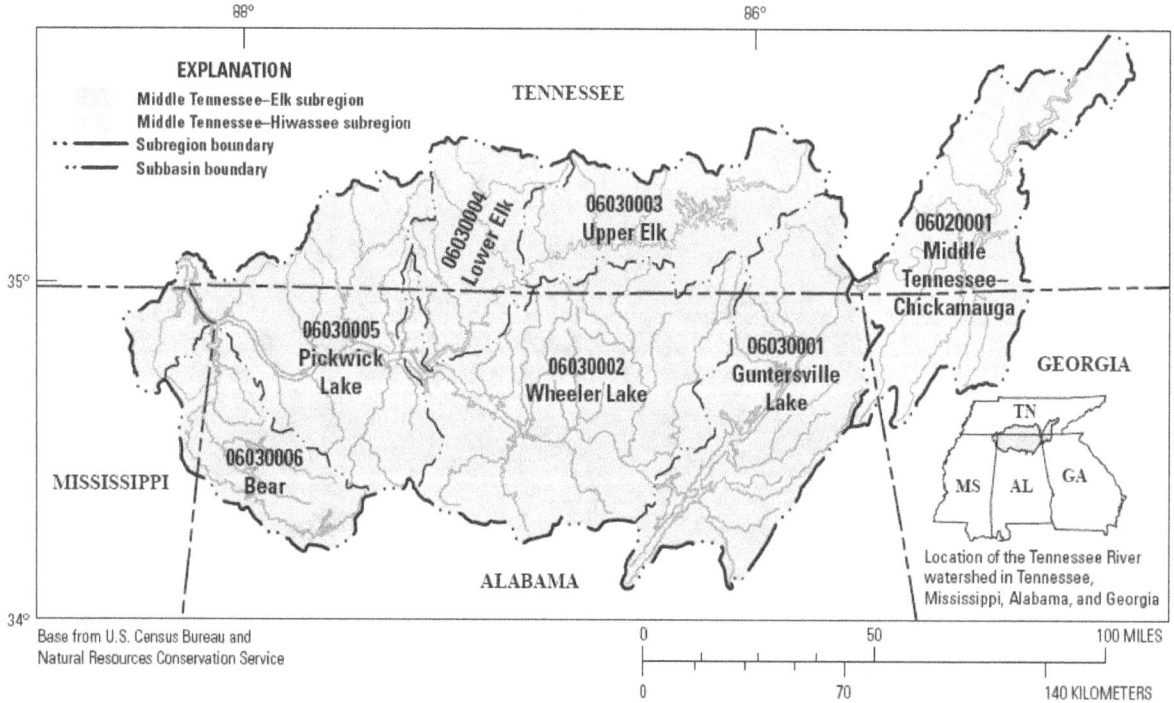

Figure 3. Subregions and subbasins of the Tennessee River watershed within Alabama.

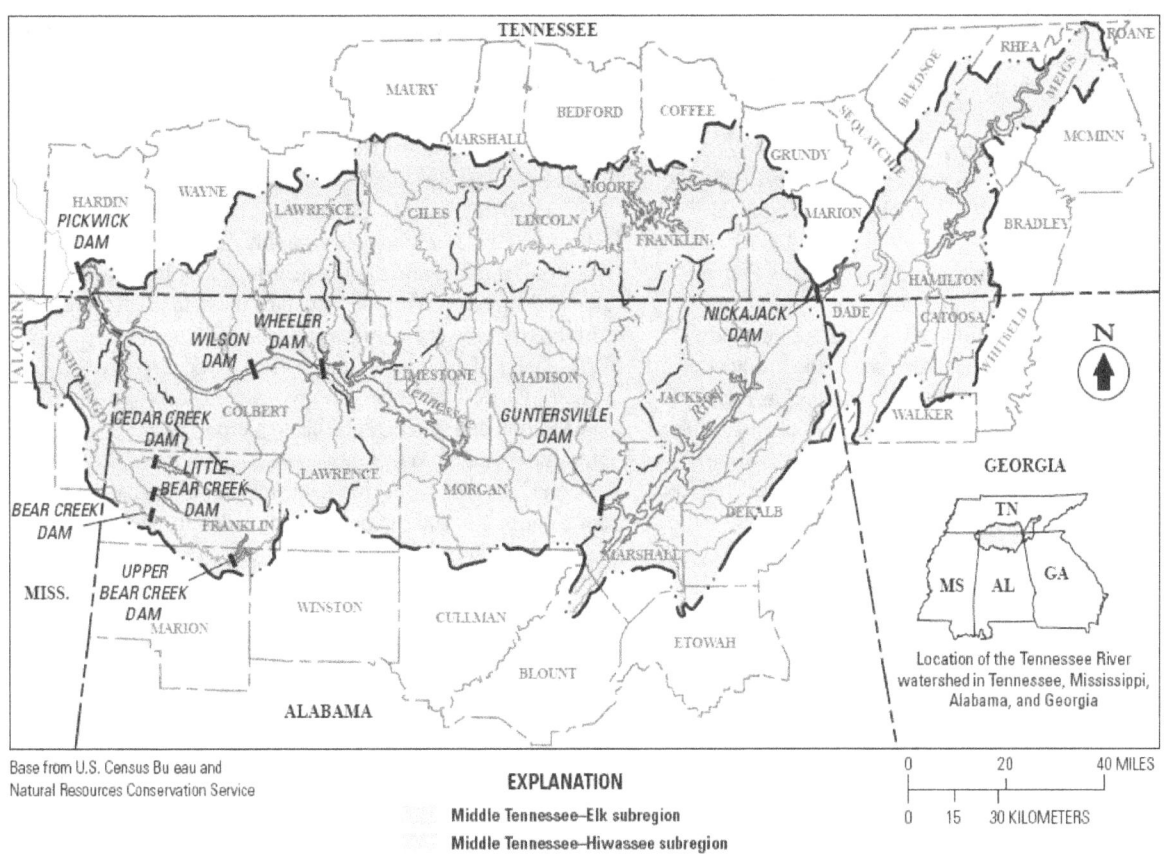

Figure 4.   Location of major dams in the Tennessee River watershed in Alabama.

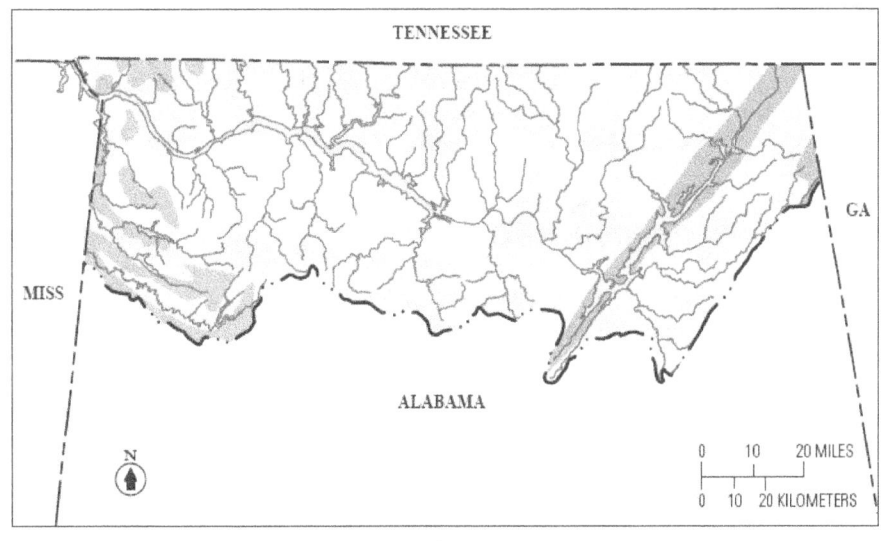

Figure 5.   Principal aquifers in the Tennessee River watershed in Alabama.

EXPLANATION

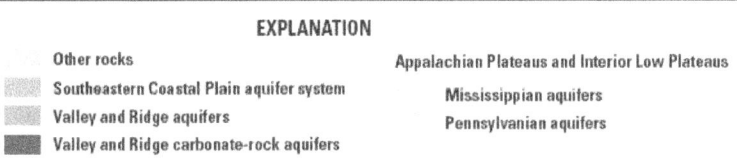

Other rocks

Southeastern Coastal Plain aquifer system

Valley and Ridge aquifers

Valley and Ridge carbonate-rock aquifers

Appalachian Plateaus and Interior Low Plateaus

Mississippian aquifers

Pennsylvanian aquifers

The Valley and Ridge aquifers are predominantly composed of limestones, dolomites, and cherts, and the groundwater production is strongly influenced by the presence of solution openings and fractures. Water stored in these solution openings may produce high well yields, but the yields are not geographically uniform across the aquifers (Bossong, 1989; Bossong and Harris, 1987; Cook and others, 2009; Miller, 1990).

In the Appalachian Plateaus and Interior Low Plateaus, many of the same limestone and dolomite formations are overlain by the Pottsville aquifer, a highly indurated and tightly cemented sandstone that crops out in the northeastern portion of the study area. The Pottsville aquifer has relatively low water yields unless local structure, such as cavities, allows for more storage; however, it can be an important source of water to domestic wells and in areas where the other aquifers are harder to access (Bossong, 1989; Cook and others, 2009; Miller, 1990).

The Tennessee River exclusively provides water to Alabama communities such as Decatur and Guntersville and supports a robust thermoelectric power generation and industrial base. Wells and springs within the Cumberland Plateau provide limited groundwater for aquaculture, industrial, mining, livestock, and self-supplied residential users (Baker, 1989; Baker and Moser, 1989; Hunter, 1991; Mooty and Richardson, 1998). Most of the groundwater use in the Tennessee River watershed is for public supply.

Table 1.   Hydrologic unit codes and names, Tennessee River watershed within Alabama.

[The map boundaries for hydrologic units are hydrographically defined, and the units are often used as a geographical framework for detailed water-resources planning. The hydrologic unit code (HUC) assigned to the hydrologic unit is an 8-digit number with each 2-digit number respectively indicating region, subregion, accounting unit, and cataloging unit. The Tennessee River watershed is designated by "06," and this table lists the seven hydrologic units in the watershed that are included, whole or in part, in Alabama. Subregion names are shown in **bold**]

Hydrologic unit code	Subregion or subbasin name
0602	**Middle Tennessee–Hiwassee**
06020001	Middle Tennessee–Chickamauga
0603	**Middle Tennessee–Elk**
06030001	Guntersville Lake
06030002	Wheeler Lake
06030003	Upper Elk
06030004	Lower Elk
06030005	Pickwick Lake
06030006	Bear

Data Compilation, Sources of Data, and Methodology

Water-use data were compiled for seven categories of water use (public supply, residential, industrial, mining, livestock, irrigation, and thermoelectric) by county and for six categories of water use (public supply, irrigation, livestock, industrial, mining, and thermoelectric) by hydrologic subregion and subbasin (table 1). Much of the data in this report is derived from results included in the statewide water-use report for Alabama (Hutson and others, 2009), a report on water availability for the Tennessee River watershed within Alabama (Cook and others, 2009), and a report about water use and water demand in the Tennessee River system (Bohac and McCall, 2008). Site-specific data were used as a basis for estimates for public supply; public-supplied deliveries; industrial, mining, and thermoelectric-power water use; and golf course, nursery, and sod irrigation. Aggregated county-level data were used as a basis for estimates for self-supplied residential uses, crop irrigation, and livestock watering. This report section contains a detailed description of the methodology and sources of data used for determining total population; public-supply and residential water-use amounts; population served and self-supplied residential population; irrigation withdrawals and irrigated acreage; livestock and mining withdrawals; and thermoelectric-power and self-supplied industrial withdrawals.

The sources and types of data are listed by water-use category in table 2. Some sources, such as the Alabama Office of Water Resources (OWR), provided site-specific water withdrawal data and source of water data for public suppliers, industries, and thermoelectric plants. Some sources, such as U.S. Department of Agriculture (USDA), provided county-level ancillary data, such as crop acreage, crop type, and crop application rate, which could be used to estimate an aggregated county irrigation water withdrawal. Some categories, such as irrigation, depended on several sources of data to estimate total water withdrawals. Sources of information are more specifically discussed in the following category sections.

The terms and units used in this report are similar to those used in previous USGS reports (MacKichan, 1951, 1957; MacKichan and Kammerer, 1961; Murray, 1968; Murray and Reeves, 1972, 1977; Solley and others, 1983, 1988, 1993, 1998; Hutson and others, 2004a, 2009). For this report, all water withdrawals were compiled as freshwater, although some low-salinity and high-salinity withdrawals for aquaculture and low-salinity withdrawals for mining occurred in the State. For 2005, water use was defined as water withdrawals for each category of use except for total residential water use. Total residential water use included public-supplied residential deliveries as well as self-supplied residential withdrawals. The term "public supplier" is the preferred term used in place of either "public water system" or "community water system." A public supplier is defined as a water system that furnishes water year-round to at least 25 people or has a minimum of 15 connections.

Table 2. Summary of data sources by water-use category and type of data for the Tennessee River watershed within Alabama.

[OWR, Alabama Department of Economic and Community Affairs, Office of Water Resources; ADEM, Alabama Department of Environmental Management; ARWA, Alabama Rural Water Association; USEPA–SDWIS, U.S. Environmental Protection Agency, Safe Drinking Water Information System; USDA–NASS, U.S. Department of Agriculture, National Agricultural Statistics Service; ADAI, Alabama Department of Agriculture and Industries; USGS–NWUIP, U.S. Geological Survey National Water-Use Information Program; DOE–EIA, U.S. Department of Energy, Energy Information Administration; TVA, Tennessee Valley Authority]

Water-use category	Data sources	Type of data
Public supply	OWR	Active public suppliers
		Monthly average-daily water withdrawals
		Source of water
		Public-supplier water deliveries by sector
	ADEM	Active public suppliers
		Monthly average-daily water withdrawals
		Source of water
	ARWA	Active public suppliers
	USEPA–SDWIS	Active and inactive public suppliers
	U.S. Census Bureau	Total population, total number of housing units, percentage of households on public supply, 1990
		Persons per household, 2000
		County population estimates, 2005
Residential	OWR	Public-supplier water deliveries by sector
	U.S. Census Bureau	Percentage of households on public supply by county, 1990
		Persons per household by county, 2000
		County population estimates, 2005
Irrigation	OWR	Source of water for crops, nurseries, and sod farms
	USDA–NASS	Irrigated acreage and crop types by county, 2002 and 2003; application rates, sprinkler system types by State, 2002 and 2003
	ADAI	Nursery and sod farm listing
	TheGolfCourses.net (2009)	Golf course listings and ancillary information
Livestock	USGS-NWUIP	County estimates of water withdrawals by source and quality of water
Mining	USGS-NWUIP	County estimates of water withdrawals by source and quality of water
Industrial	OWR	Some mine sites, monthly average-daily water withdrawals
	OWR	Water withdrawals by source of water
Thermoelectric power	DOE-EIA	Water withdrawals by source and quality of water; power generation
	OWR	Water withdrawals
	Thermoelectric power plants	Power generation
Return flows	TVA	Public supply, industrial, and thermoelectric
	OWR	Corrections to public supply, industrial, and thermoelectric

Water withdrawals are reported by county, by four-digit hydrologic subregion, and by eight-digit subbasin levels (U.S. Department of Agriculture, Soil Conservation Service, 1993; U.S. Department of Agriculture, 2004; U.S. Geological Survey, 2007b). Results are reported for all 15 counties and for 6 of the subbasins within the study area. The seventh subbasin, the Upper Elk (06030003), has an area of less than 1 mi^2 within Alabama. Estimated water use in the Upper Elk subbasin within Alabama rounded to zero for all calculated values in this report; therefore, the Upper Elk subbasin was omitted from all water-use tables and figures herein. Annual water use is expressed in terms of million gallons per day (Mgal/d). Water use is normalized as a per capita use statistic (gallons per capita per day) in five ways.

- Total water use is divided by the total population to yield **gross per capita use** and includes water used to generate electricity, support industrial and agricultural activities, and provide drinking water.

- Public-supply water use is divided by the population served by public suppliers to yield **gross public-supply per capita use** and includes water delivered to the residential, industrial, commercial, and thermoelectric power sectors and public use and losses.

- Public-supply residential deliveries are divided by the population served to yield **public-supplied residential per capita use**.

- Self-supplied residential water withdrawals are divided by self-supplied population to yield **self-supplied residential per capita use**.

- Public-supplied residential deliveries plus self-supplied residential withdrawals are divided by the total population to yield **residential per capita use**.

In the tables, State, county, subregion, subbasin, and facility data are rounded to hundredths. In the text, water withdrawal totals are reported as whole numbers unless the use of decimals is needed to improve clarity. Percentages are based on the rounded values presented in the tables and are expressed as whole numbers. All values are rounded independently; therefore, the sums of individually rounded numbers may not equal the totals given in this report.

Total Population

The 2005 estimate of population by subbasin was derived from the 2000 and 2005 county census numbers (U.S. Census Bureau, Geography Division, 2001; U.S. Census Bureau, 2006b). A county-level percentage of change in population between 2000 and 2005 was determined from reported populations. Using geographic information system (GIS) spatial techniques, the percentage of change in population was applied to

each 2000 census block group to estimate a 2005 block-group population (U.S. Census Bureau, Geography Division, 2001). The 2005 block-group population estimate then was used to calculate a population per unit area for each block group. Block groups were clipped to the subbasin by using GIS techniques, and the population per unit area for each block group was multiplied by the area of the partial block group contained within the subbasin. The resulting partial block-group populations were summed to determine a population in the areas within both the county and subbasin and then to determine the total subbasin population. Using this methodology, the total population summarized by subbasin was 0.004 percent (31 people) less than the population summarized by county. An attempt was made to balance the subbasin and county population estimates. First, populations reported for the Upper Elk hydrologic subbasin (Hydrologic Unit Code (HUC) 06030003) were removed after examination of aerial photography indicated no residences within the portion of the subbasin within the State of Alabama. Then the difference between the remaining estimates was minimized by adding people to the affected subbasins based on the proportions of county population calculated within them. A difference of one person remained after these corrections were applied. The discrepancy was due to methodology and rounding and was not adjusted further.

Populations used in this report differ somewhat from the populations reported in Hutson and others (2009) because of the difference in GIS techniques that were used to estimate population distribution. In Hutson and others (2009), block-group populations were assigned to their centroids, and in this report, the population of each block group was assumed to be evenly areally distributed. These differences in population estimates cause minor differences between the two reports in the per capita use estimates for hydrologic subbasins.

Public-Supply and Residential Water Use

For public supply, groundwater and surface-water withdrawals were reported at the county and subbasin levels, and residential deliveries and population served were estimated at the county level. Public-supply withdrawal estimates mostly were based on site-specific data (table 2). Raw-water pumpage, or the finished-water production upon which water withdrawals were estimated, was metered and reported as average-daily rates of withdrawal for each month to Alabama OWR through mandatory yearly Alabama Water Use Reporting Program (AWURP) reports and to the Drinking Water Branch–Alabama Department of Environmental Management (DWB-ADEM) through mandatory monthly operation reports (MORs). Water sold to or purchased from other public suppliers was not included in this study. To ensure that the water withdrawals were compiled for the geographical area in which the withdrawals occurred, the county and subbasin locations of the water plants, surface-water intakes, wells, or well fields were verified using GIS techniques. A comprehensive list of public suppliers was compiled from records from Alabama OWR, DWB-ADEM, Alabama Rural Water Association (ARWA), and the Internet-based Safe Drinking Water Information System (SDWIS) maintained by the U.S. Environmental Protection Agency (USEPA; U.S. Environmental Protection Agency, 2009).

For the statewide report, residential deliveries were based on a survey of the public suppliers that was conducted by Alabama OWR (Hutson and others, 2009). More than 60 percent of the suppliers responded, including all of the suppliers serving 50,000 people or more. Responses from public suppliers were used to estimate residential deliveries for public suppliers with similar demographic and geographic characteristics who had not responded. Residential deliveries were estimated at the county level from average monthly consumption for residential customers (per household use coefficient; reported by the public suppliers) in the county and the number of households in the county (calculated from U.S. Census Bureau population and persons per household data). Water withdrawals and residential deliveries were counted in the county or subbasin in which the water withdrawal occurred. Distribution areas of public suppliers were not mapped, and some deliveries may occur across county lines. Therefore, in this report, even though total public-supply withdrawals represent a summary of the best available data, significant errors in the presentation of the geographic summary of water deliveries may exist.

Residential water use is the sum of residential deliveries plus self-supplied residential withdrawals. Self-supplied residential withdrawals were not reported as part of the AWURP and were not collected as part of this study. Instead, self-supplied residential withdrawals were estimated from a self-supplied population and a per household use coefficient for each county. The self-supplied population was divided by the number of persons per household in 2000 to yield the number of self-supplied housing units in 2005. The per household use coefficients for rural households were derived from a subset of the OWR Alabama Water System Survey consisting of the small public suppliers with primarily rural residential deliveries. Self-supplied households were assumed to use the same amount of water as public-supplied rural households. For 2005, the average monthly rural household use by county ranged from 126 gallons per day (gal/d) to 300 gal/d in the Tennessee River watershed in Alabama.

Population Served and Self-Supplied Residential Population

No reliable estimates of population served by public supplier were available for 2005 (U.S. Environmental Protection Agency, 2009). Population served by public supplier, therefore, was estimated using the 1990 county census population numbers, number of housing units, and percentage of housing units on public supply (U.S. Census Bureau, 1992) and the

2005 county census population (U.S. Census Bureau, 2006a; table 2). The change in county population from 1990 to 2005 is a proxy for the change in the number of housing units on public supply during the same period. The methodology for estimating the 2005 population served assumes that any population increase from 1990 to 2005 was served by a public supplier. A simplified example of this method is as follows. The percentage of population served by public supply in the following example county increased from 60 percent in 1990 to 73 percent (11,000 population served in 2005 divided by 2005 county population, 15,000) in 2005.

For an example county in Alabama

Census Data

1990 CP	10,000
1990 HH, total	2,000
1990 $PCTHH\text{-}PS$	60
1990 $P\text{-}HH$	5
2005 CP	15,000

Calculations

$$1990\ HH\text{-}PS \qquad HH_{1990} * PCTHH\text{-}PS_{1990} \qquad (1)$$
$$1,200 \qquad 2,000 * 0.6$$

$$1990\ PP\text{-}PS \qquad HH\text{-}PS_{1990} * P\text{-}HH \qquad (2)$$
$$6,000 \qquad 1,200 * 5$$

$$2005\ PP\text{-}PS \qquad PP\text{-}PS_{1990} + (CP_{2005} - CP_{1990}) \qquad (3)$$
$$11,000 \qquad 6,000 + (15,000 - 10,000)$$

where

CP	is county population for years 1990 and 2005,
HH	is number of housing units for year 1990,
$PCTHH\text{-}PS$	is percent housing units on public supply for year 1990,
$P\text{-}HH$	is persons per housing unit for year 1990,
$HH\text{-}PS$	is number of housing units on public supply in 1990, and
$PP\text{-}PS$	is population served by public supply for years 1990 and 2005.

Self-supplied population was calculated as the difference between total county population and total county population served by public suppliers. In the case of partial counties in the Tennessee River watershed, self-supplied population was estimated in one of two ways. If one or more public suppliers were located within the partial county, then the total population was divided between public supplied and self-supplied in the same proportions as in the entire county. If no public supplier was located in the partial county, then all of the population was assumed to be self-supplied.

Irrigation

The irrigation category consists of surface-water and groundwater withdrawals for crops, nurseries, sod farms, and golf courses. At the statewide level, estimates of water withdrawals by county for crops, nurseries, and sod farms, and water withdrawals for golf courses were derived independently using data from multiple sources (Hutson and others, 2009). For this report, county-level irrigation withdrawals were estimated by multiplying the percentage of total county area contained within the Tennessee River watershed by the total county withdrawals reported in Hutson and others (2009). County-level withdrawals for irrigation were reported for the total irrigated lands, which were not specified by type.

Livestock and Mining

In this report, county-level water withdrawals by source for livestock were modified from estimates determined by the USGS National Water-Use Information Program (NWUIP) because livestock withdrawals are not reported as a specific category within the AWURP and site-specific data were not collected as part of this study. For the NWUIP, estimates of livestock withdrawals by county were calculated from the 2005 livestock census by the U.S. Department of Agriculture, National Agricultural Statistics Service (USDA-NASS) and from statewide drinking water-requirement coefficients for individual livestock types (Kammerer, 1976; Mooty and Richardson, 1998). The coefficients do not reflect the effect of climate on animal watering across the State or facility maintenance needs. In this report, NWUIP estimates were used for counties entirely contained within the Tennessee River watershed. Livestock water-use estimates for partial counties were made by multiplying livestock water use for the entire county by the percentage of county area contained within the Tennessee River watershed. For source estimation in partial counties, groundwater and surface-water sources of water used for livestock were assumed to account for the same percentages of water use as in the entire county.

Water withdrawals for livestock by subbasin were determined by applying GIS techniques. The subbasin boundaries were superimposed on the county boundaries to create a subbasin/county areal unit. Each subbasin/county unit represents a percentage of the subbasin area within a county. Surface-water and groundwater withdrawals were distributed among the subbasin/county units based on the assigned areal percentage. Water withdrawals for each subbasin/county unit were summarized by subbasin. Total groundwater withdrawal estimates by county were 0.01 Mgal/d greater than total groundwater withdrawal estimates by subbasin. No attempt was made to make the county and subbasin total withdrawal estimates equal because the difference in totals was due to methodology and rounding differences between the two estimates.

County-level water withdrawals by source for mining were modified from estimates determined by the USGS NWUIP and site-specific data from the AWURP. Mining water use was estimated from per ton water-use coefficients and crude ore production in tons for 2004 from the USGS Minerals Information Team, from coal production in tons from the U.S. Department of Energy, Energy Information Administration (DOE-EIA), and from site-specific mining withdrawal data reported to the AWURP. Mining water-use estimates for partial counties in the Tennessee River watershed were made by multiplying mining water use for the entire county by the percentage of county area contained within the Tennessee River watershed. Mining water-use estimates were available at the county level only, so for source estimation in partial counties, groundwater and surface-water sources were assumed to account for the same percentages of water use as in the entire county.

Thermoelectric Power and Industrial

Thermoelectric power and industrial water use were estimated from site-specific data. The primary sources of data for thermoelectric power water withdrawals and power produced were the DOE-EIA, the AWURP database eWater, and the individual thermoelectric power facilities (table 2). Water withdrawals were reported in the county or subbasin in which the withdrawals occurred.

The AWURP database, eWater, stores monthly average- daily water withdrawals, source of water, and location information. For 2005, steam-electric plants with a nameplate capacity of 100 megawatts or more provided information about cooling type, water withdrawal, return flow, and consumptive use by generating unit (except for nuclear power plants) to DOE-EIA, and all power plants provided power generation by generating unit (Energy Information Administration, 2008, 2009a, 2009b).

Monthly self-supplied industrial withdrawals by source were reported by individual industries to the AWURP for 2005. Standard Industrial Classification (SIC) codes for those industries were obtained from the Alabama Directory of Manufacturers (Alabama Development Office, 2004). Public-supplied industrial deliveries were not available at the watershed level.

Return Flow and Net Water Demand

Return flow is water returned to a groundwater or surface-water source after release from the point of use. Return flow data for public supply, self-supplied industrial, and thermoelectric water uses were compiled and reported by the TVA. Data were checked and revised where necessary to reflect more detailed data available in ADECA-OWR files. Livestock and irrigation water uses were assumed to be entirely consumptive. Data were not available for return flows from self-supplied residential and mining water uses, so these uses were also treated in this report as entirely consumptive. Net water demand is the difference between a water withdrawal and the associated return flow. Return flow and net water demand totals by county and subbasin have been incorporated into the water-use tables in this report.

Water Use

Total Water Use

Total water use in the Tennessee River watershed within Alabama for 2005 was determined from estimates of water withdrawals for seven categories—public supply (including deliveries to the other water use categories), residential, irrigation, livestock, industrial, mining, and thermoelectric power (fig. 6). All seven categories were estimated for the counties in the watershed, and all categories except self-supplied residential were estimated for hydrologic units in the watershed. Reported total water use by hydrologic unit is less than the reported total by county because it does not include the estimate for self-supplied residential water use (tables 3 and 4). For 2005, all withdrawals in the Tennessee River watershed were considered to be freshwater. Total withdrawals were estimated to be 5,197 Mgal/d (table 3). Estimates of withdrawals by source indicate that total surface-water withdrawals were 99 percent of the total (5,139 Mgal/d), and the remaining 1 percent was from groundwater (58 Mgal/d; fig. 7). Gross per capita use averaged 6,056 gal/d for the 858,097 residents in the Alabama portion of the Tennessee River watershed (U.S. Census Bureau, 2006a). Gross per capita use is the total water withdrawn divided by the total population. The large per capita use is a result of the large thermoelectric power withdrawals in relation to the population size. Total residential water use, which is a combination of residential deliveries from public supply and self-supplied residential withdrawals, was about 75 Mgal/d (see the "Residential" section in this report).

The geographic distributions of total, groundwater, and surface-water withdrawals by county and by hydrologic subbasin are shown in figures 8 and 9. The largest total water withdrawals occurred in Limestone, Jackson, and Colbert Counties. Withdrawals in these counties were approximately 94 percent of the total withdrawals in the study area and were primarily used for the cooling needs at thermoelectric power plants. Excluding thermoelectric power, the largest withdrawals occurred in Morgan, Madison, Colbert, and Lawrence Counties (table 5).

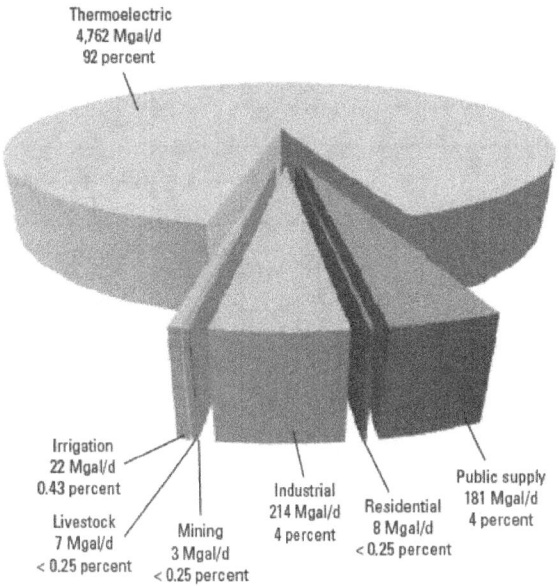

Figure 6. Comparison of freshwater withdrawals by category of use in the Tennessee River watershed within Alabama, 2005.

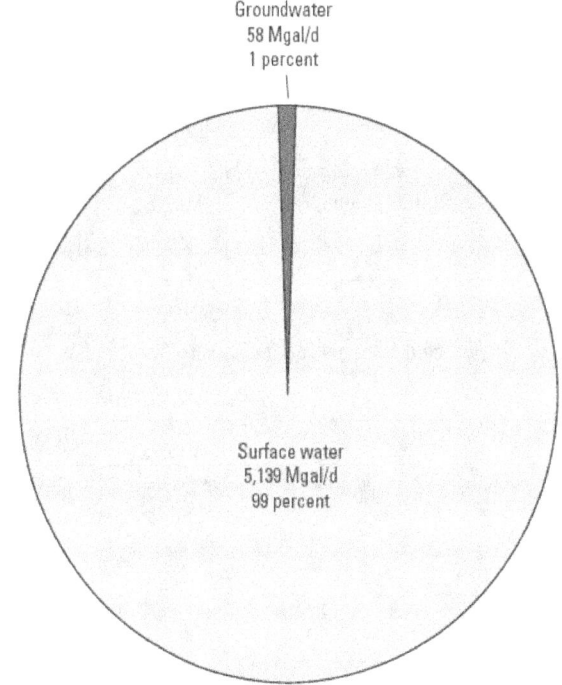

Figure 7. Sources of water used in the Tennessee River watershed in Alabama, 2005.

Table 3. Total freshwater withdrawals and consumption by source and county in the Tennessee River watershed within Alabama, 2005.

[Figures may not sum to totals because of independent rounding; County names in **bold** type indicate counties entirely contained in the watershed]

County	Withdrawals, in million gallons per day			Return flows, in million gallons per day	Consumption, in million gallons per day
	Groundwater	Surface water	Total		Net water demand
Blount	0.17	0.04	0.21	0.00	0.21
Colbert	3.54	1,359.60	1,363.14	1,350.67	12.47
Cullman	0.40	0.07	0.47	0.00	0.47
DeKalb	2.65	2.00	4.65	0.00	4.65
Etowah	0.24	0.05	0.29	0.00	0.29
Franklin	2.07	4.66	6.73	3.71	3.02
Jackson	1.97	1,496.26	1,498.23	1,489.64	8.59
Lauderdale	3.64	13.50	17.14	9.68	7.46
Lawrence	1.21	65.70	66.91	53.50	13.41
Limestone	6.01	2,006.00	2,012.01	1,993.62	18.39
Madison	28.94	43.45	72.39	37.21	35.18
Marion	0.13	3.20	3.33	0.12	3.21
Marshall	4.01	22.33	26.34	10.46	15.88
Morgan	2.41	122.29	124.70	112.68	12.02
Winston	0.15	0.01	0.16	0.00	0.16
Total	**57.54**	**5,139.16**	**5,196.70**	**5,061.29**	**135.73**

Table 4. Total freshwater withdrawals and consumption by source and by hydrologic subregion and subbasin in the Tennessee River watershed within Alabama, 2005.

[Figures may not sum to totals because of independent rounding]

Hydrologic subregion and subbasin		Withdrawals, in million gallons per day			Return flows, in million gallons per day	Consumption, in million gallons per day
		Groundwater	Surface water	Total		Net water demand
Middle Tennessee–Hiwassee						
06020001	Middle Tennessee–Chickamauga	0.77	0.16	0.93	0.00	0.93
Subtotal		*0.77*	*0.16*	*0.93*	*0.00*	*0.93*
Middle Tennessee–Elk						
06030001	Guntersville Lake	5.58	1,519.87	1,525.45	1,499.09	26.36
06030002	Wheeler Lake	35.62	2,224.02	2,259.64	2,197.07	62.57
06030004	Lower Elk	0.81	11.43	12.24	0.11	12.13
06030005	Pickwick Lake	4.99	1,375.38	1,380.37	1,361.18	19.19
06030006	Bear	2.01	8.29	10.30	3.83	6.47
Subtotal		*49.01*	*5,138.99*	*5,188.00*	*5,061.28*	*126.72*
Total		**49.78**	**5,139.15**	**5,188.93**	**5,061.28**	**127.65**

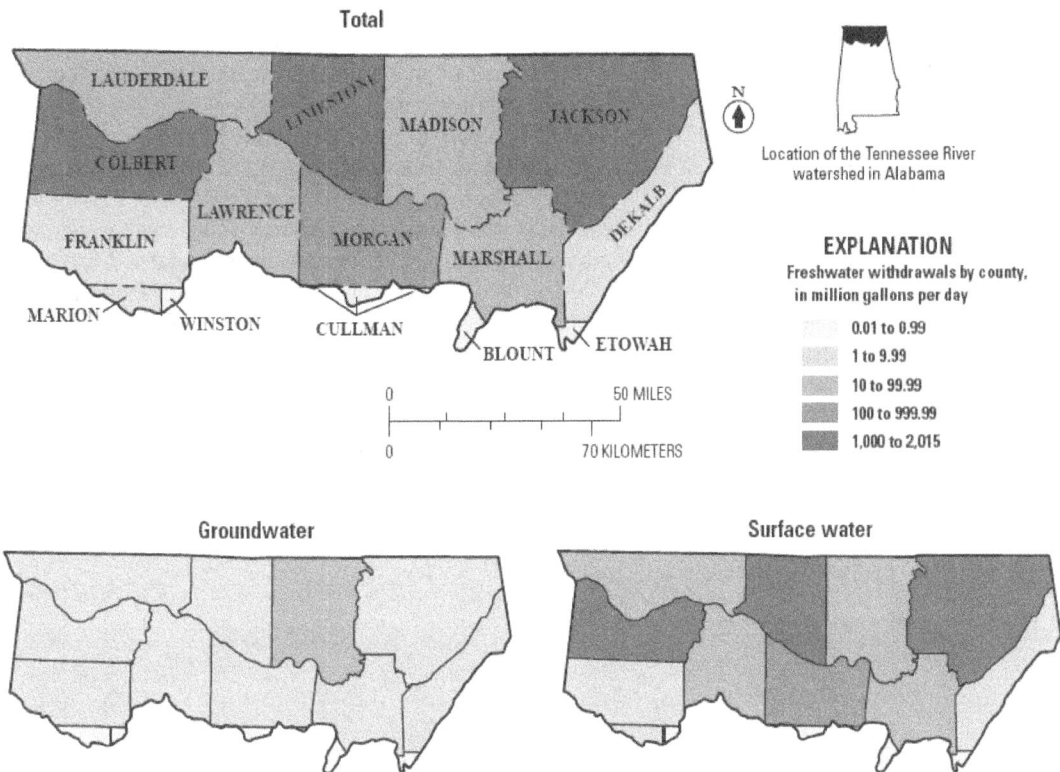

Figure 8. Total freshwater withdrawals by source and county in the Tennessee River watershed in Alabama, 2005.

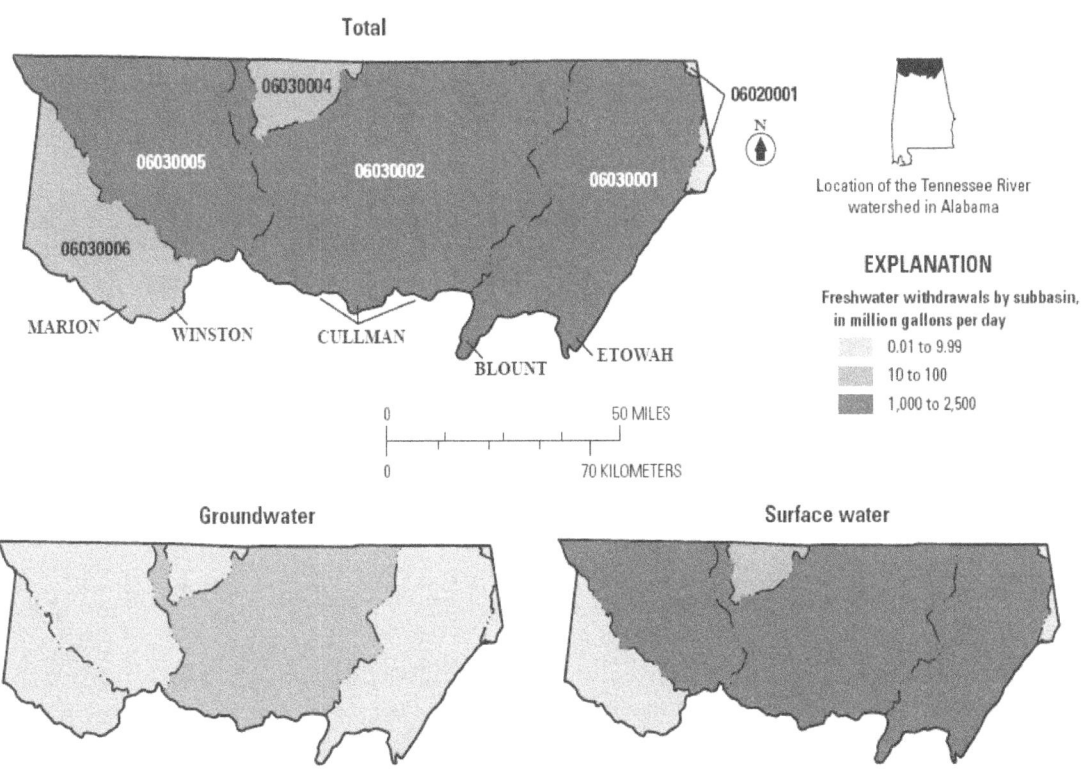

Figure 9. Total freshwater withdrawals by source and hydrologic subbasin in the Tennessee River watershed in Alabama, 2005.

Total withdrawals by source and category for counties and hydrologic subbasins are listed in tables 3–6. For 2005, thermoelectric power accounted for 92 percent of the total water withdrawals, or 4,762 Mgal/d (tables 5 and 6; fig. 6). Combined, the public-supply and self-supplied industrial categories accounted for about 8 percent of the total withdrawals (181 Mgal/d and 214 Mgal/d, respectively), and irrigation, self-supplied residential, livestock, and mining accounted for the remaining less than 1 percent. More surface water than groundwater was used in all categories except mining and self-supplied residential (tables 7–10). About 93 percent of the surface-water withdrawals were for thermoelectric power, and the largest surface-water withdrawals were in Limestone County (table 7). About 95 percent of the surface-water withdrawals—primarily used for thermoelectric power—occurred in Limestone, Jackson, Colbert Counties in the Middle Tennessee–Elk subregion (tables 7 and 8). Most of the groundwater withdrawals, 62 percent, were used for public supply (tables 9 and 10). About 50 percent (29 Mgal/d) of the watershed-wide groundwater use was in Madison County; most of that water (88 percent) was used for public supply.

Estimates of public-supply, irrigation, livestock, self-supplied industrial, mining, and thermoelectric power withdrawals by source of water for hydrologic subregion and subbasin and are listed in tables 6, 8, and 10. These categories accounted for more than 99 percent (5,189 Mgal/d) of the total estimated withdrawals. The exclusion of the small withdrawal amounts for self-supplied residential (8 Mgal/d in 2005) by subbasin does not affect the understanding of the overall distribution pattern of water use in the Tennessee River watershed in Alabama. The Middle Tennessee–Elk subregion accounted for almost all of the 5,189 Mgal/d total estimated withdrawals. About 92 percent of that water was for thermoelectric power, and nearly all of the water was surface water. The second largest use category in the Tennessee River watershed was self-supplied industrial, which accounted for about 50 percent (214 Mgal/d) of the nonpower water withdrawal.

Table 5. Total freshwater withdrawals by category of use and county in the Tennessee River watershed within Alabama, 2005.

[Figures may not sum to totals because of independent rounding. County names in **bold** type indicate counties entirely contained in the watershed]

County	Withdrawals, in million gallons per day								
	Public supply	**Residential**	**Irrigation**	**Livestock**	**Industrial**	**Mining**	**Subtotal without thermoelectric**	**Thermoelectric**	**Total**
Blount	0.00	0.10	0.03	0.04	0.00	0.04	0.21	0.00	0.21
Colbert	9.56	0.31	2.34	0.30	56.44	0.05	69.00	1,294.14	1,363.14
Cullman	0.00	0.28	0.07	0.12	0.00	0.00	0.47	0.00	0.47
DeKalb	1.17	0.87	1.38	1.23	0.00	0.00	4.65	0.00	4.65
Etowah	0.00	0.23	0.04	0.02	0.00	0.00	0.29	0.00	0.29
Franklin	4.70	0.31	0.45	0.70	0.00	0.57	6.73	0.00	6.73
Jackson	10.71	0.91	0.71	0.72	8.78	0.10	21.93	1,476.30	1,498.23
Lauderdale	14.19	1.30	1.17	0.48	0.00	0.00	17.14	0.00	17.14
Lawrence	6.91	0.47	1.49	0.63	57.18	0.23	66.91	0.00	66.91
Limestone	11.52	1.05	8.26	0.44	0.00	0.50	21.77	1,990.24	2,012.01
Madison	64.44	1.12	4.91	0.33	0.89	0.70	72.39	0.00	72.39
Marion	3.17	0.11	0.01	0.04	0.00	0.00	3.33	0.00	3.33
Marshall	24.14	0.29	0.57	1.02	0.04	0.28	26.34	0.00	26.34
Morgan	30.42	0.30	0.86	0.73	90.65	0.54	123.50	1.20	124.70
Winston	0.00	0.14	0.00	0.02	0.00	0.00	0.16	0.00	0.16
Total	**180.93**	**7.78**	**22.29**	**6.82**	**213.98**	**3.01**	**434.81**	**4,761.88**	**5,196.69**

Table 6. Total freshwater withdrawals by category of use and hydrologic subregion and subbasin in the Tennessee River watershed within Alabama, 2005.

[Figures may not sum to totals because of independent rounding. All values are in million gallons per day]

Hydrologic subregion and subbasin		Withdrawals, in million gallons per day							
		Public supply	**Irrigation**	**Livestock**	**Industrial**	**Mining**	**Subtotal without thermoelectric**	**Thermo-electric**	**Total**
Middle Tennessee–Hiwassee									
06020001	Middle Tennessee–Chickamauga	0.66	0.14	0.13	0.00	0.00	0.93	0.00	1.86
Subtotal		*0.66*	*0.14*	*0.13*	*0.00*	*0.00*	*0.93*	*0.00*	*1.86*
Middle Tennessee–Elk									
06030001	Guntersville Lake	35.38	2.22	2.37	8.82	0.36	49.15	1,476.30	1,574.60
06030002	Wheeler Lake	103.13	12.62	2.34	148.72	1.39	268.20	1,991.44	2,527.84
06030004	Lower Elk	8.84	2.72	0.18	0.00	0.50	12.24	0.00	24.48
06030005	Pickwick Lake	25.07	3.42	1.04	56.44	0.26	86.23	1,294.14	1,466.60
06030006	Bear	7.87	1.17	0.75	0.00	0.51	10.30	0.00	20.60
Subtotal		*180.29*	*22.15*	*6.68*	*213.98*	*3.02*	*426.12*	*4,761.88*	*5,614.12*
Total		**180.95**	**22.29**	**6.81**	**213.98**	**3.02**	**427.05**	**4,761.88**	**5,615.98**

Table 7.   Total surface-water withdrawals by category of use and county in the Tennessee River watershed within Alabama, 2005.

[Figures may not sum to totals because of independent rounding. County names in **bold** type indicate counties that are entirely contained within the watershed]

County	Surface-water withdrawals, in million gallons per day						
	Public supply	**Irrigation**	**Livestock**	**Industrial**	**Mining**	**Thermoelectric**	**Total**
Blount	0.00	0.02	0.02	0.00	0.00	0.00	0.04
Colbert	8.27	1.40	0.17	55.57	0.05	1,294.14	1,359.60
Cullman	0.00	0.01	0.06	0.00	0.00	0.00	0.07
DeKalb	0.47	0.88	0.65	0.00	0.00	0.00	2.00
Etowah	0.00	0.04	0.01	0.00	0.00	0.00	0.05
Franklin	3.88	0.20	0.40	0.00	0.18	0.00	4.66
Jackson	10.08	0.67	0.40	8.78	0.03	1,476.30	1,496.26
Lauderdale	12.79	0.43	0.28	0.00	0.00	0.00	13.50
Lawrence	6.91	1.18	0.36	57.18	0.07	0.00	65.70
Limestone	8.85	6.16	0.25	0.00	0.50	1,990.24	2,006.00
Madison	38.85	3.30	0.19	0.89	0.22	0.00	43.45
Marion	3.17	0.01	0.02	0.00	0.00	0.00	3.20
Marshall	21.16	0.57	0.51	0.00	0.09	0.00	22.33
Morgan	30.42	0.74	0.40	89.36	0.17	1.20	122.29
Winston	0.00	0.00	0.01	0.00	0.00	0.00	0.01
Total	**144.85**	**15.61**	**3.73**	**211.78**	**1.31**	**4,761.88**	**5,139.16**

Table 8.   Total surface-water withdrawals by category of use and hydrologic subregion and subbasin in the Tennessee River watershed within Alabama, 2005.

[Figures may not sum to totals because of independent rounding]

Hydrologic subregion and subbasin		Surface-water withdrawals, in million gallons per day						
		Public supply	**Irrigation**	**Livestock**	**Industrial**	**Mining**	**Thermo-electric**	**Total**
Middle Tennessee–Hiwassee								
06020001	Middle Tennessee–Chickamauga	0.00	0.09	0.07	0.00	0.00	0.00	0.16
Subtotal		0.00	0.09	0.07	0.00	0.00	0.00	0.16
Middle Tennessee–Elk								
06030001	Guntersville Lake	31.72	1.72	1.25	8.78	0.10	1,476.30	1,519.87
06030002	Wheeler Lake	74.26	9.17	1.28	147.43	0.44	1,991.44	2,224.02
06030004	Lower Elk	8.84	1.99	0.10	0.00	0.50	0.00	11.43
06030005	Pickwick Lake	22.98	1.98	0.60	55.57	0.11	1,294.14	1,375.38
06030006	Bear	7.05	0.64	0.43	0.00	0.17	0.00	8.29
Subtotal		*144.85*	*15.50*	*3.66*	*211.78*	*1.32*	*4,761.88*	*5,138.99*
Total		**144.85**	**15.59**	**3.73**	**211.78**	**1.32**	**4,761.88**	**5,139.15**

Table 9. Total groundwater withdrawals by category of use and county in the Tennessee River watershed within Alabama, 2005.

[Figures may not sum to totals because of independent rounding. County names in **bold** type indicate counties entirely contained within the watershed]

County	Groundwater withdrawals, in million gallons per day						
	Public supply	**Residential**	**Irrigation**	**Livestock**	**Industrial**	**Mining**	**Total**
Blount	0.00	0.10	0.01	0.02	0.00	0.04	0.17
Colbert	1.29	0.31	0.94	0.13	0.87	0.00	3.54
Cullman	0.00	0.28	0.06	0.06	0.00	0.00	0.40
De Kalb	0.70	0.87	0.50	0.58	0.00	0.00	2.65
Etowah	0.00	0.23	0.00	0.01	0.00	0.00	0.24
Franklin	0.82	0.31	0.25	0.30	0.00	0.39	2.07
Jackson	0.63	0.91	0.04	0.32	0.00	0.07	1.97
Lauderdale	1.40	1.30	0.74	0.20	0.00	0.00	3.64
Lawrence	0.00	0.47	0.31	0.27	0.00	0.16	1.21
Limestone	2.67	1.05	2.10	0.19	0.00	0.00	6.01
Madison	25.59	1.12	1.61	0.14	0.00	0.48	28.94
Marion	0.00	0.11	0.00	0.02	0.00	0.00	0.13
Marshall	2.98	0.29	0.00	0.51	0.04	0.19	4.01
Morgan	0.00	0.30	0.12	0.33	1.29	0.37	2.41
Winston	0.00	0.14	0.00	0.01	0.00	0.00	0.15
Total	**36.08**	**7.78**	**6.68**	**3.09**	**2.20**	**1.70**	**57.54**

Table 10. Total groundwater withdrawals by category of use and hydrologic subregion and subbasin in the Tennessee River watershed within Alabama, 2005.

[Figures may not sum to totals because of independent rounding]

Hydrologic subregion and subbasin		Groundwater withdrawals, in million gallons per day					
		Public supply	**Irrigation**	**Livestock**	**Industrial**	**Mining**	**Total**
Middle Tennessee–Hiwassee							
06020001	Middle Tennessee–Chickamauga	0.66	0.05	0.06	0.00	0.00	0.77
Subtotal		*0.66*	*0.05*	*0.06*	*0.00*	*0.00*	*0.77*
Middle Tennessee–Elk							
06030001	Guntersville Lake	3.66	0.50	1.12	0.04	0.26	5.58
06030002	Wheeler Lake	28.87	3.45	1.06	1.29	0.95	35.62
06030004	Lower Elk	0.00	0.73	0.08	0.00	0.00	0.81
06030005	Pickwick Lake	2.09	1.44	0.44	0.87	0.15	4.99
06030006	Bear	0.82	0.53	0.32	0.00	0.34	2.01
Subtotal		*35.44*	*6.65*	*3.02*	*2.20*	*1.70*	*49.01*
Total		**36.10**	**6.70**	**3.08**	**2.20**	**1.70**	**49.78**

Public Supply

Public supply refers to water that is withdrawn, treated, and distributed by public suppliers. Public suppliers provide water for a variety of uses, such as residential, commercial, industrial, thermoelectric-power, and public-water use. Thermoelectric power deliveries, industrial/commercial deliveries, and public uses and losses were not estimated separately but are included in the total public-supply withdrawals in this report.

Public-supply data are listed by county in table 11 and by hydrologic subbasin in table 12. For 2005, public-supply withdrawals in the Tennessee River watershed in Alabama were 181 Mgal/d. Public-supply withdrawals were 3.5 percent of total withdrawals and about 42 percent of total withdrawals for all categories excluding thermoelectric power (table 5). The majority of the public-supply water (145 Mgal/d, or 80 percent) was withdrawn from surface-water sources

(fig. 10). The remaining 36 Mgal/d, or 20 percent, was withdrawn from wells and springs. In 2005, about 765,000 people, or 89 percent of the population, depended on water from public suppliers.

The geographic distributions of the total, groundwater, and surface-water withdrawals for public supply by county are shown in figure 11. Madison County, which encompasses the city of Huntsville, had the largest amount of withdrawal, accounting for about 36 percent of the public-supply withdrawals in the Tennessee River Valley in Alabama (figs. 11 and 12, table 11). Public suppliers in Colbert, Madison, Marshall, and Morgan Counties collectively served more than 90 percent of their respective county populations (table 11). The largest surface-water withdrawals occurred in Madison and Morgan Counties (39 and 30 Mgal/d, respectively), and the largest groundwater withdrawals occurred in Madison County (26 Mgal/d).

Table 11.   Public-supply population served, withdrawals, per capita use, return flows, and consumption by county in the Tennessee River watershed in Alabama, 2005.

[Figures may not sum to totals because of independent rounding. County names in **bold** type indicate counties entirely contained within the Tennessee River Watershed]

County	Population	Population served by public supply		Withdrawals by source, in million gallons per day			Gross public supply per capita use, in gallons per day	Return flow, in million gallons per day	Consumption, in million gallons per day
		Total	Percentage	Ground-water	Surface water	Total			Net water demand
Blount	1,600	0[1]	0	0.00	0.00	0.00	—	0.00	0.00
Colbert	54,660	50,704	93	1.29	8.27	9.56	189	4.44	5.12
Cullman	3,401	0[1]	0	0.00	0.00	0.00	—	0.00	0.00
De Kalb	40,330	29,346	73	0.70	0.47	1.17	40	0.00	1.17
Etowah	2,840	0[1]	0	0.00	0.00	0.00	—	0.00	0.00
Franklin	28,458	22,450	79	0.82	3.88	4.7	209	3.71	0.99
Jackson	53,650	39,924	74	0.63	10.08	10.71	268	5.24	5.47
Lauderdale	87,691	73,713	84	1.40	12.79	14.19	192	9.68	4.51
Lawrence	33,193	27,892	84	0.00	6.91	6.91	248	1.30	5.61
Limestone	70,469	59,659	85	2.67	8.85	11.52	193	6.02	5.50
Madison	298,192	288,901	97	25.59	38.85	64.44	223	36.27	28.17
Marion	3,473	2,357	68	0.00	3.17	3.17	1,345	0.12	3.05
Marshall	63,989	59,832	94	2.98	21.16	24.14	403	10.30	13.84
Morgan	113,510	109,690	97	0.00	30.42	30.42	277	21.79	8.63
Winston	2,641	0[1]	0	0.00	0.00	0.00	—	0.00	0.00
Total	**858,097**	**764,468**	**89**	**36.08**	**144.85**	**180.93**	**237**	**98.87**	**82.06**

[1] No public water-supply withdrawals were reported in the portion of this county within the Tennessee River watershed in 2005. All estimated population for this area was assumed to be self-supplied. Distribution areas of local public water supplies were not determined for this study, and there may be some error in the assumption that the entire population of these areas is self-supplied.

Table 12.   Public-supply water use by hydrologic subregion and subbasin in the Tennessee River watershed within Alabama, 2005.

[Figures may not sum to totals because of independent rounding]

Hydrologic subregion and subbasin		Total population	Withdrawals by source, in million gallons per day			Return flow, in million gallons per day	Consumption, in million gallons per day
			Groundwater	Surface water	Total	day	Net water demand
Middle Tennessee–Hiwassee							
06020001	Middle Tennessee–Chickamauga	2,519	0.66	0.00	0.66	0.00	0.66
Subtotal		*2,519*	*0.66*	*0.00*	*0.66*	*0.00*	*0.66*
Middle Tennessee–Elk							
06030001	Guntersville Lake	137,739	3.66	31.72	35.38	14.69	20.69
06030002	Wheeler Lake	517,460	28.87	74.26	103.13	65.30	37.83
06030004	Lower Elk	15,440	0.00	8.84	8.84	0.11	8.73
06030005	Pickwick Lake	152,409	2.09	22.98	25.07	14.96	10.11
06030006	Bear	32,530	0.82	7.05	7.87	3.83	4.04
Subtotal		*855,578*	*35.44*	*144.85*	*180.29*	*98.89*	*81.40*
Total		**858,097**	**36.10**	**144.85**	**180.95**	**98.89**	**82.06**

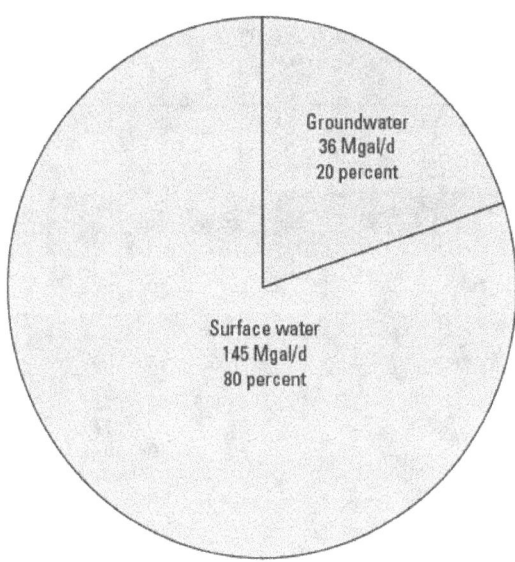

Figure 10.   Source of public-supply water withdrawals in the Tennessee River watershed in Alabama, 2005.

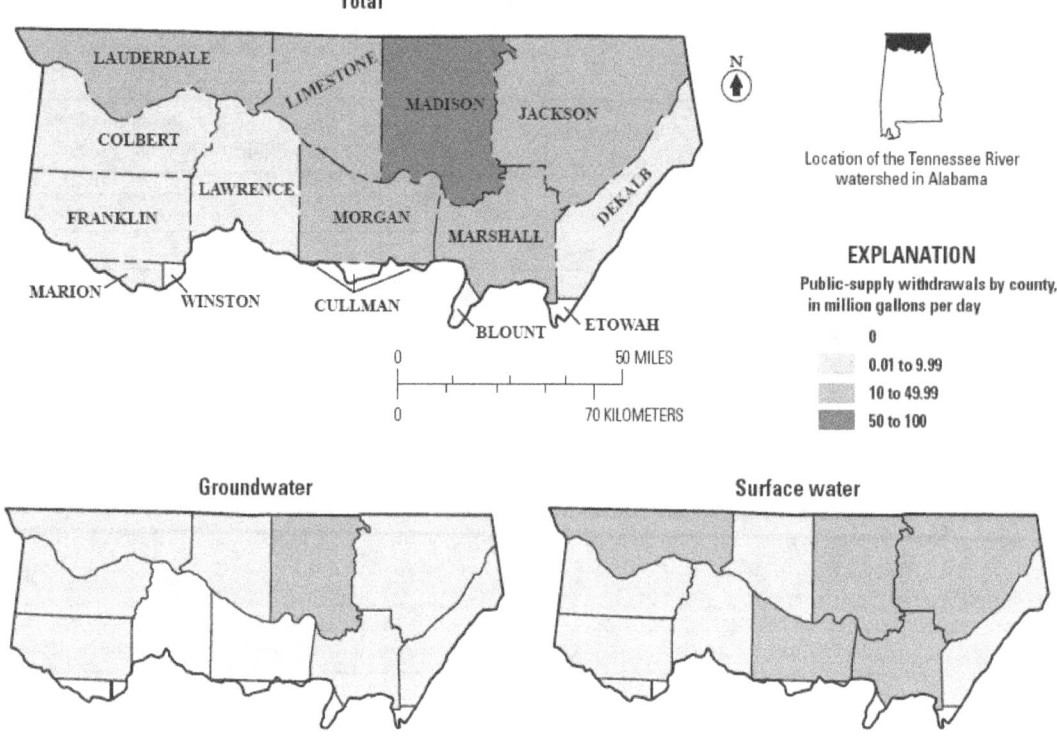

Figure 11. Public-supply freshwater withdrawals by source and county in the Tennessee River watershed in Alabama, 2005.

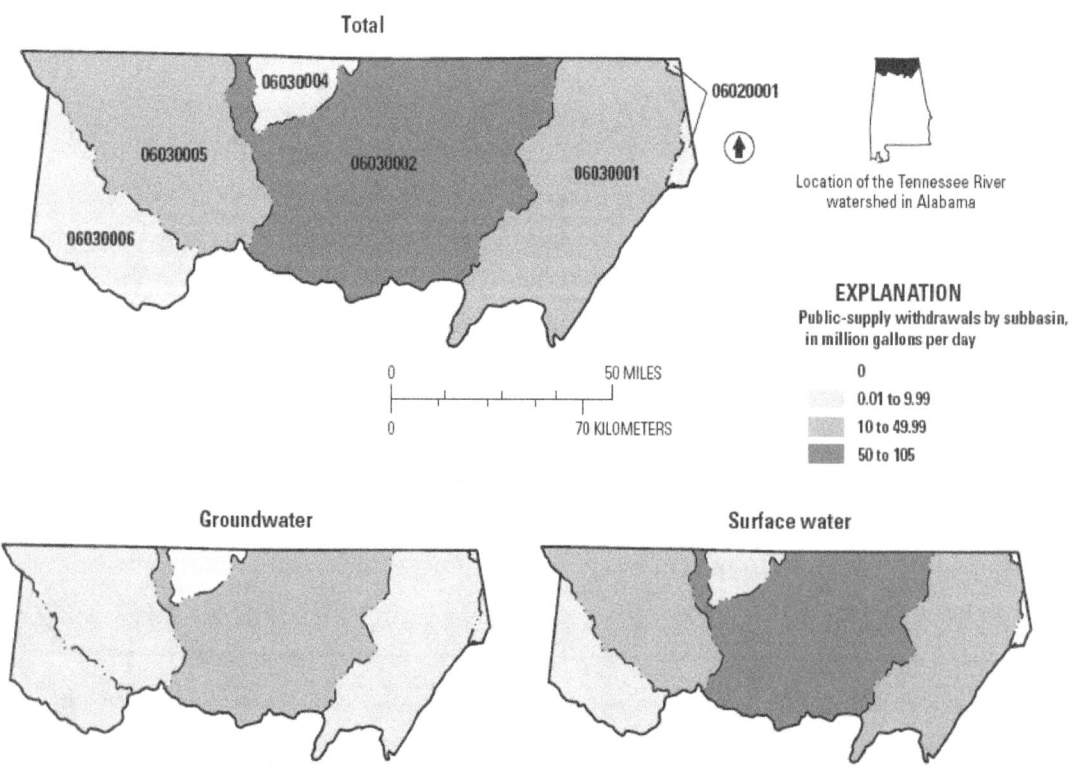

Figure 12. Public-supply freshwater withdrawals by source and subbasin in the Tennessee River watershed in Alabama, 2005.

Residential

Residential water refers to the water that is used for all indoor household purposes, such as drinking, preparing food, bathing, washing clothes and dishes, and flushing toilets, and outdoor purposes, such as watering lawns and gardens and pool maintenance. Residential water use is defined in this report as public-supplied residential deliveries plus self-supplied residential withdrawals. Residential water use in the Tennessee River watershed totaled 75 Mgal/d in 2005 (table 13). Public suppliers delivered 90 percent, or 67 Mgal/d, of residential water, while the remaining 10 percent, or 8 Mgal/d, of residential water was self-supplied from private groundwater wells. Self-supplied residential withdrawals were less than 1 percent of the total water withdrawals and about 2 percent of the withdrawals for all categories except thermo-electric power (table 5). About 11 percent of the population (or 93,629 people) relied on private wells for their drinking-water needs in 2005 (table 13).

The geographic distributions of groundwater withdrawals for self-supplied residential use, self-supplied residential population as a percentage of the total Tennessee River watershed population, and self-supplied residential population by county are shown in figures 13 and 14. The largest aggregated self-supplied residential withdrawals were in Lauderdale (1.30 Mgal/d) and Madison (1.12 Mgal/d) Counties (table 13). These two counties represented about 31 percent of the total self-supplied residential withdrawals and 25 percent of the self-supplied residential population.

Table 13. Residential water users, water use, and per capita use by county in the Tennessee River watershed within Alabama, 2005.

[Figures may not sum to totals because of independent rounding. County names in **bold** type indicate counties entirely contained within the watershed]

County	Population			Residential water use, in million gallons per day			Residential per capita use, in gallons per day		
	Total	Served by public supply	Self-supplied	Withdrawals	Deliveries	Total	Self-supplied[1]	Public-supplied	Combined
Blount	1,600	0[2]	1,600	0.10	0.00	0.10	62	—[3]	62
Colbert	54,660	50,704	3,956	0.31	3.31	3.61	77	65	66
Cullman	3,401	0[2]	3,401	0.28	0.00	0.28	81	—[3]	81
DeKalb	40,330	29,346	10,984	0.87	2.96	3.83	79	101	95
Etowah	2,840	0[2]	2,840	0.23	0.00	0.23	82	—[3]	82
Franklin	28,458	22,450	6,008	0.31	1.43	1.74	51	64	61
Jackson	53,650	39,924	13,726	0.91	2.69	3.60	67	67	67
Lauderdale	87,691	73,713	13,978	1.30	6.01	7.31	93	82	83
Lawrence	33,193	27,892	5,301	0.47	2.27	2.74	89	81	83
Limestone	70,469	59,659	10,810	1.05	4.25	5.30	97	71	75
Madison	298,192	288,901	9,291	1.12	30.91	32.03	121	107	107
Marion	3,473	2,357	1,116	0.11	0.20	0.31	95	84	88
Marshall	63,989	59,832	4,157	0.29	4.02	4.31	69	67	67
Morgan	113,510	109,690	3,820	0.30	9.07	9.38	79	83	83
Winston	2,641	0[2]	2,641	0.14	0.00	0.14	51	—[3]	51
Total	**858,097**	**764,468**	**93,629**	**7.78**	**67.11**	**74.89**			
Percent		**89**	**11**						
Average							80	79	77

[1] Per capita use was calculated by dividing total withdrawals by the self-supplied population.

[2] No public water-supply withdrawals were reported in the portion of this county within the Tennessee River watershed in 2005. All estimated population for this area was assumed to be self-supplied. Distribution areas of local public water supplies were not determined for this study, and there may be some error in the assumption that the entire population of these areas is self-supplied.

[3] Public-supplied residential per capita use was not estimated because no public water-supply withdrawals were reported in the portion of the county located within the Tennessee River watershed.

Total (groundwater)

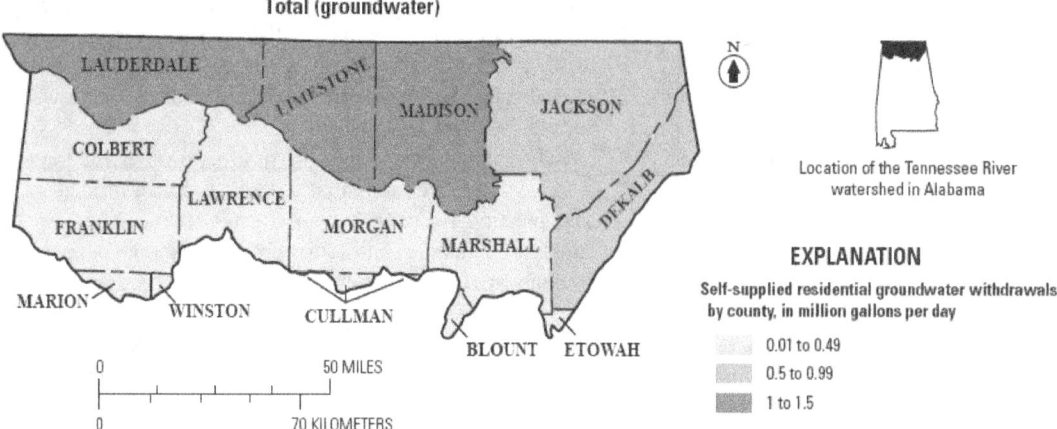

Figure 13.   Self-supplied residential groundwater withdrawals by county in the Tennessee River watershed in Alabama, 2005.

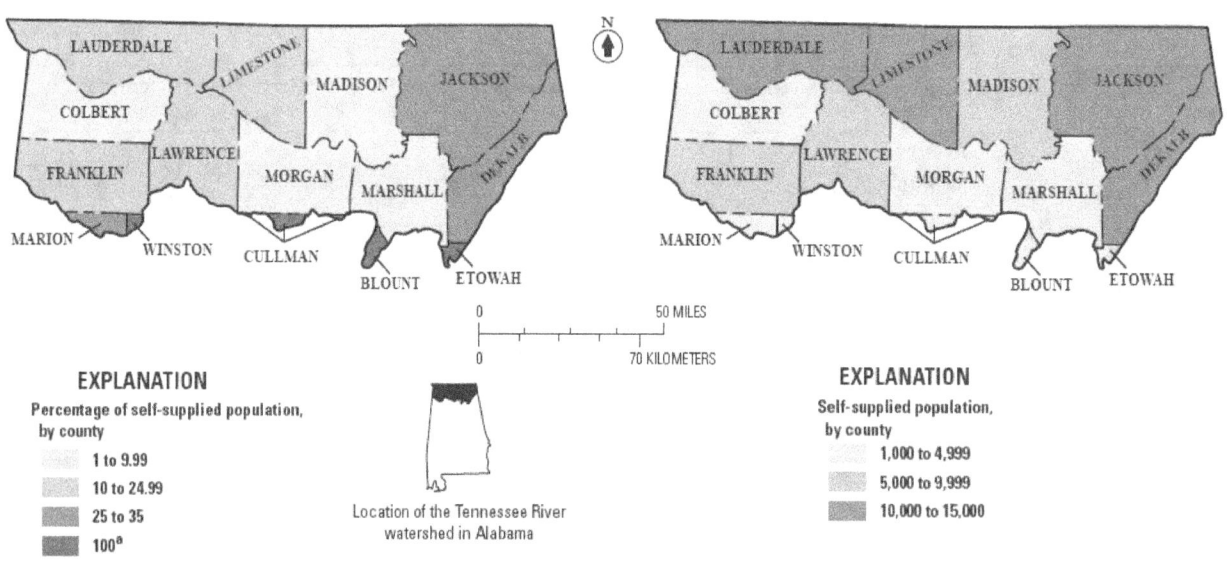

Figure 14.   Self-supplied residential population as a percentage of total population and self-supplied residential population by county in the Tennessee River watershed in Alabama, 2005.

The average residential per capita use in the study area—public-supplied residential deliveries plus self-supplied residential withdrawals divided by the total population—was 77 gal/d (table 13). The average public-supplied residential per capita use in the study area—public-supplied residential deliveries divided by population served—was 79 gal/d and ranged from 64 gal/d for Franklin County to 107 gal/d for Madison County. Public-supplied residential per capita use was not calculated for the portions of Blount, Cullman, Etowah, and Winston Counties in the Tennessee River watershed because no public suppliers were known to be located in those areas. Instead, all populations in those partial counties were assumed

to be self-supplied. The average self-supplied residential per capita use in the study area—self-supplied residential withdrawals divided by self-supplied residential population—was 80 gal/d.

The sources of information and methodology for estimating public-supply residential deliveries, population served by public suppliers, self-supplied residential withdrawals, and self-supplied population are detailed in the "Public-Supply and Residential Water Use" and "Population Served and Self-Supplied Residential Population" sections in the "Data Compilation, Sources of Data, and Methodology" section of this report.

Irrigation

Irrigation water refers to water that is applied by an irrigation system to assist in the growing of crops and pastures or to maintain vegetative growth in recreational lands such as parks and golf courses. Irrigation includes water that is applied for pre-irrigation, frost protection, chemical application, weed control, field preparation, crop cooling, harvesting, dust suppression, and the leaching of salts from the root zone and water that is lost in conveyance. Conveyance loss was not reported for 2005. Although annual water-use data are expressed in terms of million gallons per day, irrigation water is applied, generally, only during part of each year and at variable rates; therefore, the actual rate of application during the growing season would be more than the daily rate expressed as million gallons per day.

Irrigation withdrawals and irrigated acreage by county and subbasin are listed in tables 14 and 15, respectively. For 2005, total irrigation withdrawals for the Tennessee River watershed in Alabama were 22 Mgal/d. Irrigation withdrawals were less than 1 percent of total withdrawals and about 5 percent of total withdrawals for all categories excluding thermoelectric power (table 5). Of the total irrigation withdrawals, 70 percent, or 16 Mgal/d, was from surface water, and the remaining 30 percent, or 7 Mgal/d, was from groundwater (table 14; fig. 15). Consumptive use of all irrigation withdrawals is estimated to be 100 percent in 2005. Acres of irrigated land in partial counties and the total irrigation water withdrawn by county were calculated by multiplying amounts for entire counties by the percentage of the county within the Tennessee River watershed.

Table 14.   Irrigation water use by county in the Tennessee River watershed in Alabama, 2005.

[Figures may not sum to totals because of independent rounding. County names in **bold** type indicate counties entirely contained within the watershed]

County	Estimated irrigated acreage within the Tennessee River watershed, in thousand acres	Withdrawals, in million gallons per day			Return flow, in million gallons per day	Consumption, in million gallons per day
		Groundwater	Surface water	Total		Net water demand
Blount	0.02	0.01	0.02	0.03	0.00	0.03
Colbert	2.64	0.94	1.40	2.34	0.00	2.34
Cullman	0.04	0.06	0.01	0.07	0.00	0.07
DeKalb	0.74	0.50	0.88	1.38	0.00	1.38
Etowah	0.05	0.00	0.04	0.04	0.00	0.04
Franklin	0.51	0.25	0.20	0.45	0.00	0.45
Jackson	0.95	0.04	0.67	0.71	0.00	0.71
Lauderdale	1.16	0.74	0.43	1.17	0.00	1.17
Lawrence	1.97	0.31	1.18	1.49	0.00	1.49
Limestone	8.74	2.10	6.16	8.26	0.00	8.26
Madison	5.56	1.61	3.30	4.91	0.00	4.91
Marion	0.01	0.00	0.01	0.01	0.00	0.01
Marshall	1.08	0.00	0.57	0.57	0.00	0.57
Morgan	1.39	0.12	0.74	0.86	0.00	0.86
Winston	0.00	0.00	0.00	0.00	0.00	0.00
Total	**24.87**	**6.68**	**15.61**	**22.29**	**0.00**	**22.29**

Table 15.   Irrigation water use by hydrologic subregion and subbasin in the Tennessee River watershed within Alabama, 2005.

[Figures may not sum to totals because of independent rounding]

Hydrologic subregion and subbasin		Withdrawals, in million gallons per day			Return flow, in million gallons per day	Consumption, in million gallons per day
		Groundwater	Surface water	Total		Net water demand
Middle Tennessee–Hiwassee						
06020001	Middle Tennessee–Chickamauga	0.05	0.09	0.14	0.00	0.14
Subtotal		*0.05*	*0.09*	*0.14*	*0.00*	*0.14*
Middle Tennessee–Elk						
06030001	Guntersville Lake	0.50	1.72	2.22	0.00	2.22
06030002	Wheeler Lake	3.45	9.17	12.62	0.00	12.62
06030004	Lower Elk	0.73	1.99	2.72	0.00	2.72
06030005	Pickwick Lake	1.44	1.98	3.42	0.00	3.42
06030006	Bear	0.53	0.64	1.17	0.00	1.17
Subtotal		*6.65*	*15.50*	*22.15*	*0.00*	*22.15*
Total		**6.70**	**15.59**	**22.29**	**0.00**	**22.29**

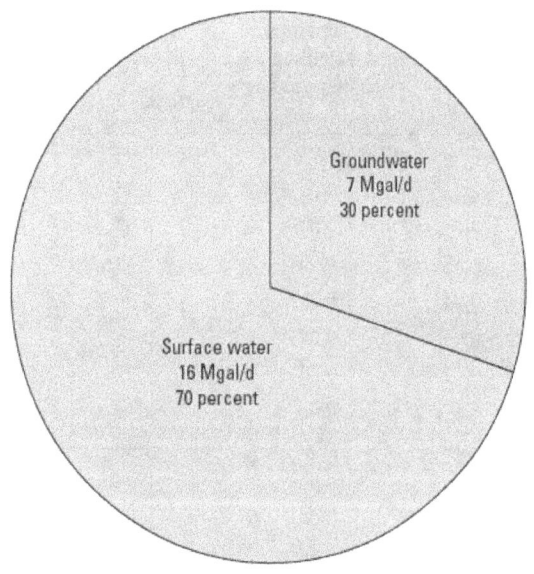

The geographic distributions of total, groundwater, and surface-water withdrawals for irrigation by county and by hydrologic subbasin are shown in figures 16 and 17, respectively. Nine of the 15 counties withdrew less than 1 Mgal/d each for irrigation. Limestone County withdrew 37 percent (8 Mgal/d) of the irrigation water (table 14). Six counties (Colbert, DeKalb, Lauderdale, Lawrence, Limestone, and Madison) each had withdrawals of more than 1 Mgal/d, for a total withdrawal of 20 Mgal/d or nearly 88 percent of the irrigation total for the Tennessee River watershed in Alabama. The Wheeler Lake subbasin (HUC 06030002, in the Middle Tennessee-Elk subregion) had the greatest withdrawal for irrigation, 13 Mgal/d, which is about 57 percent of the total withdrawals for irrigation (table 15).

Figure 15.   Source of water for irrigation use in the Tennessee River Watershed in Alabama, 2005. (Mgal/d, million gallons per day)

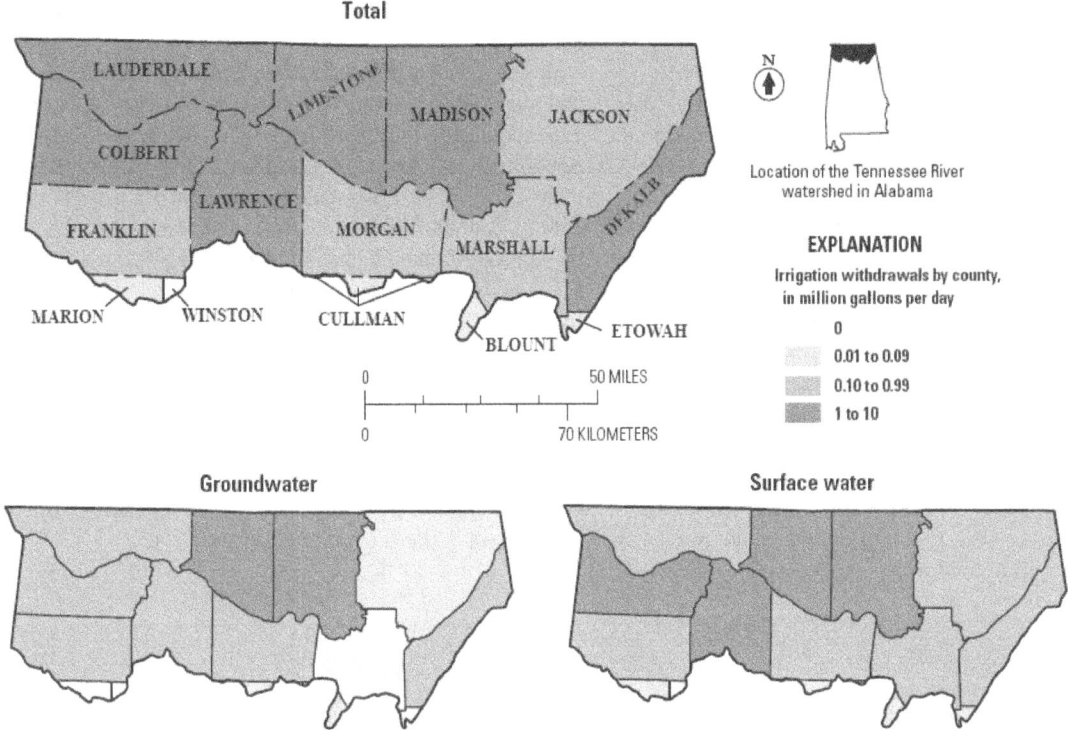

Figure 16.   Irrigation withdrawals by source and county in the Tennessee River watershed in Alabama, 2005.

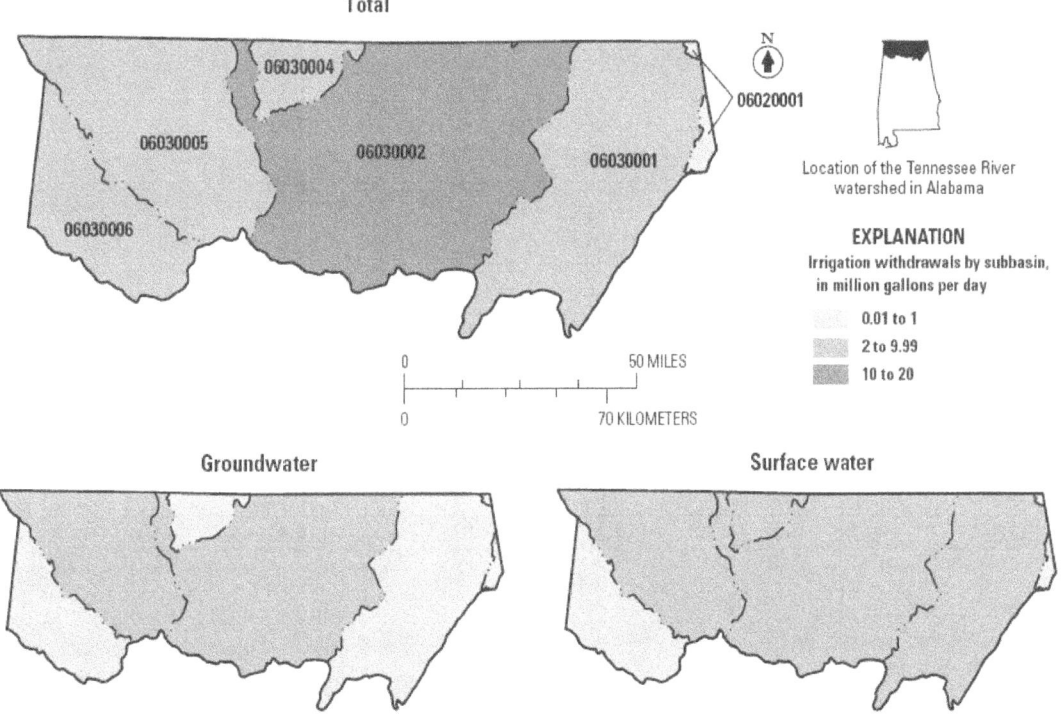

Figure 17.   Irrigation withdrawals by source and subbasin in the Tennessee River watershed in Alabama, 2005.

Livestock

Livestock water use is associated with livestock watering, feedlots, dairy operations, and other on-farm needs. Water consumed by cooling of the facilities for the animals and products, dairy sanitation and cleaning of facilities, animal waste-disposal systems, and incidental water loss during livestock care is included within the livestock water use category. The primary livestock types in Alabama include poultry, beef cattle and calves, dairy cows and heifers, hogs and pigs, and horses and ponies. The livestock category excludes on-farm residential use (residential category) and irrigation water use.

During 2005, withdrawals for livestock in the Tennessee River watershed in Alabama were 7 Mgal/d (tables 16 and 17). Surface water was the source for 55 percent (4 Mgal/d) of the withdrawals, and groundwater was the source for the remaining 45 percent (3 Mgal/d) (fig. 18). Withdrawals of water for livestock use were less than 1 percent of total withdrawals and were nearly 2 percent of total withdrawals excluding thermo-electric power (table 5).

The geographic distributions of total, groundwater, and surface-water withdrawals for livestock by county and by hydrologic subbasin are shown in figures 19 and 20. The counties with large water withdrawals for livestock mostly corresponded to the areas of Alabama with major producers of poultry, cattle and calves, and hogs and pigs (U.S. Department of Agriculture, National Agricultural Statistics Service, 2006a). Blount, Cullman, DeKalb, and Marshall Counties, the top four broiler chicken producing counties in Alabama, accounted for about 35 percent of the total withdrawals for livestock (U.S. Department of Agriculture, National Agricultural Statistics Service, 2006b). The Guntersville Lake (2.4 Mgal/d), Wheeler Lake (2.3 Mgal/d), and Pickwick Lake (1 Mgal/d) subbasins accounted for 84 percent (6 Mgal/d) of the total withdrawals for livestock in the Tennessee River watershed in Alabama. These three subbasins also encompass the portions of Blount, Cullman, DeKalb, and Marshall Counties that are within the Tennessee River watershed.

Table 16.   Water withdrawals for livestock by county in the Tennessee River watershed within Alabama, 2005.

[Figures may not sum to totals because of independent rounding. County names in **bold** type indicate counties entirely contained within the watershed]

County	Withdrawals, in million gallons per day			Consumption, in million gallons per day
	Groundwater	Surface water	Total	Net water demand
Blount	0.02	0.02	0.04	0.04
Colbert	0.13	0.17	0.30	0.30
Cullman	0.06	0.06	0.12	0.12
DeKalb	0.58	0.65	1.23	1.23
Etowah	0.01	0.01	0.02	0.02
Franklin	0.30	0.4	0.70	0.70
Jackson	0.32	0.4	0.72	0.72
Lauderdale	0.20	0.28	0.48	0.48
Lawrence	0.27	0.36	0.63	0.63
Limestone	0.19	0.25	0.44	0.44
Madison	0.14	0.19	0.33	0.33
Marion	0.02	0.02	0.04	0.04
Marshall	0.51	0.51	1.02	1.02
Morgan	0.33	0.4	0.73	0.73
Winston	0.01	0.01	0.02	0.02
Total	**3.09**	**3.73**	**6.82**	**6.82**

Table 17. Water withdrawals for livestock by hydrologic subregion and subbasin in Tennessee River watershed within Alabama, 2005.

[Figures may not sum to totals because of independent rounding]

Hydrologic subregion and subbasin		Withdrawals, in million gallons per day			Consumption, in million gallons per day
		Groundwater	Surface water	Total	Net water demand
Middle Tennessee–Hiwassee					
06020001	Middle Tennessee–Chickamauga	0.06	0.07	0.13	0.13
Subtotal		*0.06*	*0.07*	*0.13*	*0.13*
Middle Tennessee–Elk					
06030001	Guntersville Lake	1.12	1.25	2.37	2.37
06030002	Wheeler Lake	1.06	1.28	2.34	2.34
06030004	Lower Elk	0.08	0.10	0.18	0.18
06030005	Pickwick Lake	0.44	0.60	1.04	1.04
06030006	Bear	0.32	0.43	0.75	0.75
Subtotal		*3.02*	*3.66*	*6.68*	*6.68*
Total		**3.08**	**3.73**	**6.81**	**6.81**

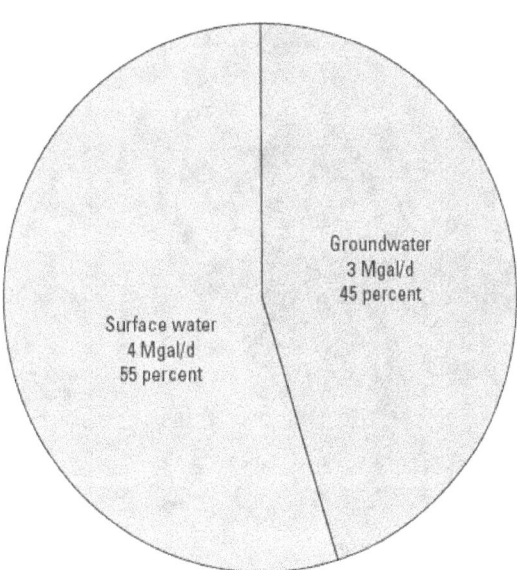

Figure 18. Source of water for livestock use in the Tennessee River watershed in Alabama, 2005.

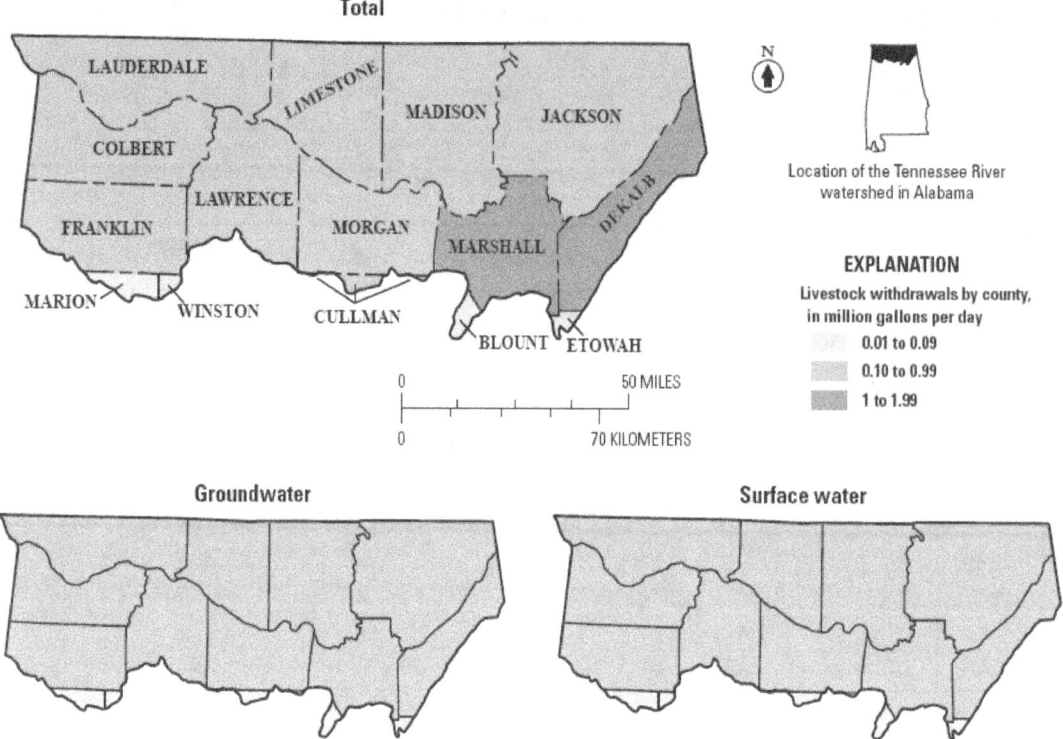

Figure 19.   Withdrawals for livestock by source and county in the Tennessee River watershed in Alabama, 2005.

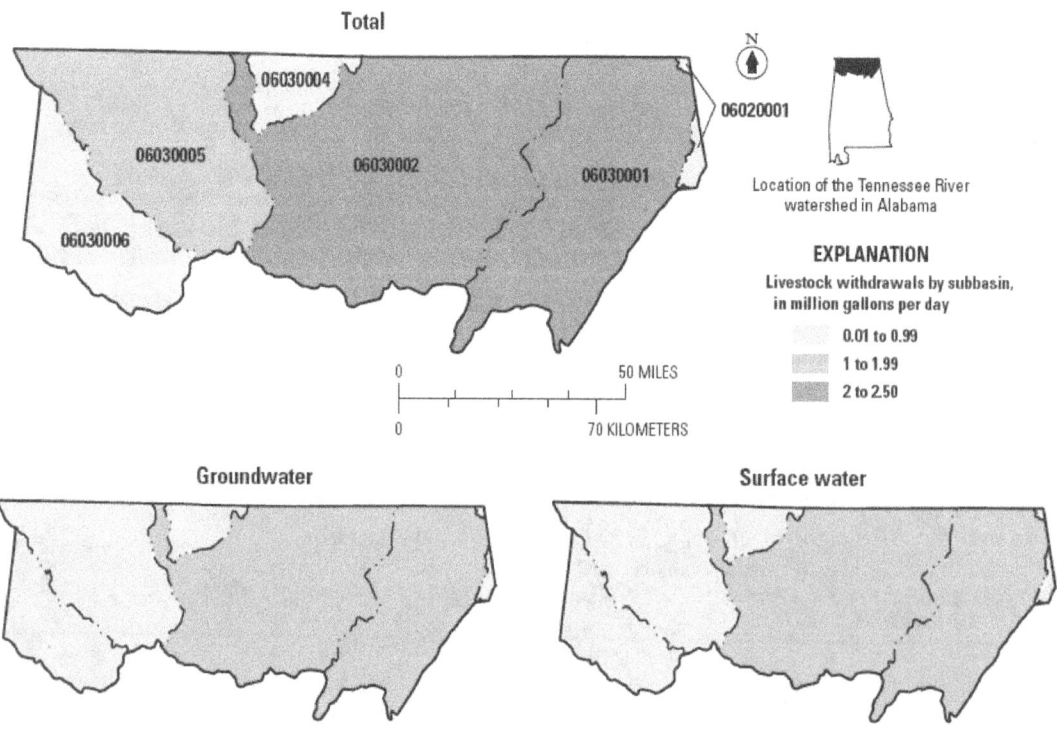

Figure 20.   Withdrawals for livestock by source and subbasin in the Tennessee River watershed in Alabama, 2005.

Self-Supplied Industrial

Industrial water is water used for fabrication, processing, washing, and cooling and includes such industries as chemical and allied products, food, paper and allied products, petroleum refining, and steel. Industries can purchase water from a public supply, be self-supplied, or both. Estimates of public-supplied industrial water deliveries were not made for the Tennessee River watershed in Alabama in 2005. Site-specific information reported to the AWURP was used to calculate self-supplied industrial water use in the watershed.

Self-supplied industrial withdrawals are listed by county and by hydrologic subbasin in tables 18 and 19, respectively. For 2005, self-supplied industrial withdrawals in the Tennessee River watershed in Alabama were 214 Mgal/d, which is about 4 percent of total withdrawals and about 49 percent of total withdrawals excluding thermoelectric power (table 5). Surface water was the source for 99 percent (212 Mgal/d) of the withdrawals, and groundwater was the source of the remaining 1 percent (2 Mgal/d; fig. 21).

The geographic distributions of total, groundwater, and surface-water withdrawals for self-supplied industrial use by county and by hydrologic subbasin are shown in figures 22 and 23, respectively. Withdrawals for self-supplied industrial use occurred in only 6 of the 15 counties. The largest withdrawals occurred in Morgan, Colbert (primarily chemical and allied products), and Lawrence Counties with withdrawals that were more than 50 Mgal/d each. Withdrawals in these counties accounted for about 95 percent (204 Mgal/d) of the total self-supplied industrial withdrawals.

No industrial withdrawals were reported in the Middle Tennessee–Hiwassee subregion. In the Middle Tennessee–Elk hydrologic subregion, most industrial withdrawals were made by the chemical, paper, and the allied industries (table19; fig. 24). Within the Middle Tennessee–Elk hydrologic subregion, the largest total self-supplied industrial withdrawals occurred in the Wheeler Lake (HUC 06030002) and Pickwick Lake (HUC 06030005) subbasins (table 19).

Table 18. Self-supplied industrial water withdrawals, returns, and net demand by county in the Tennessee River watershed within Alabama, 2005.

[Figures may not sum to totals because of independent rounding. County names in **bold** indicate counties entirely contained within the watershed]

County	Withdrawals, in million gallons per day			Return flows, in million gallons per day	Consumption, in million gallons per day
	Groundwater	Surface water	Total		Net Demand
Blount	0.00	0.00	0.00	0.00	0.00
Colbert	0.87	55.57	56.44	53.39	3.05
Cullman	0.00	0.00	0.00	0.00	0.00
DeKalb	0.00	0.00	0.00	0.00	0.00
Etowah	0.00	0.00	0.00	0.00	0.00
Franklin	0.00	0.00	0.00	0.00	0.00
Jackson	0.00	8.78	8.78	8.12	0.66
Lauderdale	0.00	0.00	0.00	0.00	0.00
Lawrence	0.00	57.18	57.18	52.20	4.98
Limestone	0.00	0.00	0.00	0.06	-0.06
Madison	0.00	0.89	0.89	0.93	-0.04
Marion	0.00	0.00	0.00	0.00	0.00
Marshall	0.04	0	0.04	0.15	-0.11
Morgan	1.29	89.36	90.65	90.48	0.17
Winston	0.00	0.00	0.00	0.00	0.00
Total	**2.20**	**211.78**	**213.98**	**205.34**	**8.65**

Table 19.   Self-supplied industrial water withdrawals, returns, and net demands by hydrologic subregion and subbasin in the Tennessee River watershed within Alabama, 2005.

[Figures may not sum to totals because of independent rounding]

Hydrologic subregion and subbasin		Withdrawals, in million gallons per day			Return flow, in million gallons per day	Consumption, in million gallons per day
		Groundwater	Surface water	Total		Net water demand
Middle Tennessee–Hiwassee						
06020001	Middle Tennessee–Chickamauga	0	0	0.00	0.00	0.00
Subtotal		*0*	*0*	*0.00*	*0.00*	*0.00*
Middle Tennessee–Elk						
06030001	Guntersville Lake	0.04	8.78	8.82	8.12	0.70
06030002	Wheeler Lake	1.29	147.43	148.72	143.83	4.89
06030004	Lower Elk	0.00	0.00	0.00	0.00	—
06030005	Pickwick Lake	0.87	55.57	56.44	53.39	3.05
06030006	Bear	0.00	0.00	0.00	0.00	—
Subtotal		*2.20*	*211.78*	*213.98*	*205.34*	*8.64*
Total		**2.20**	**211.78**	**213.98**	**205.34**	**8.64**

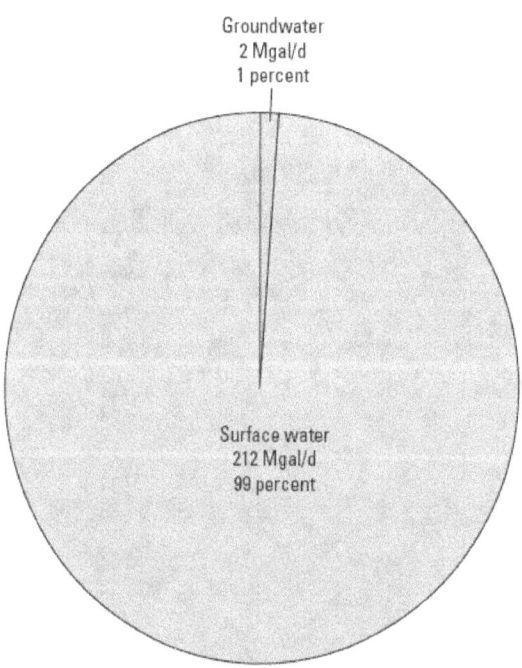

Groundwater
2 Mgal/d
1 percent

Surface water
212 Mgal/d
99 percent

Figure 21.   Source of water for self-supplied industrial use in the Tennessee River watershed in Alabama, 2005.

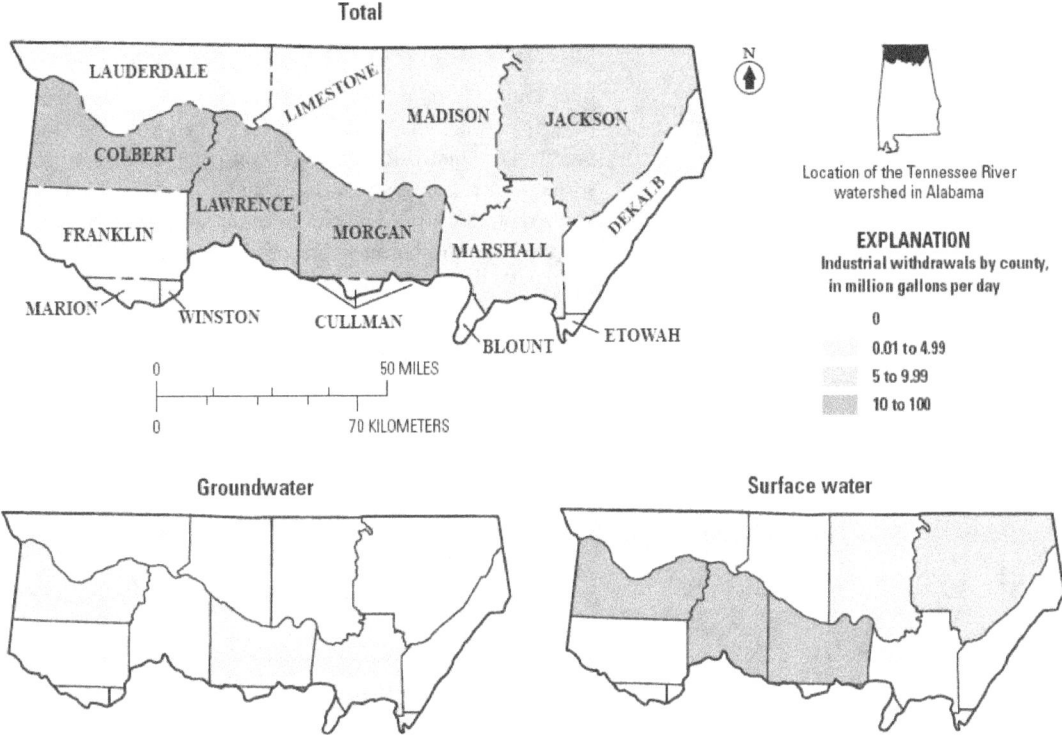

Figure 22.   Self-supplied industrial freshwater withdrawals by source and county in the Tennessee River watershed in Alabama, 2005.

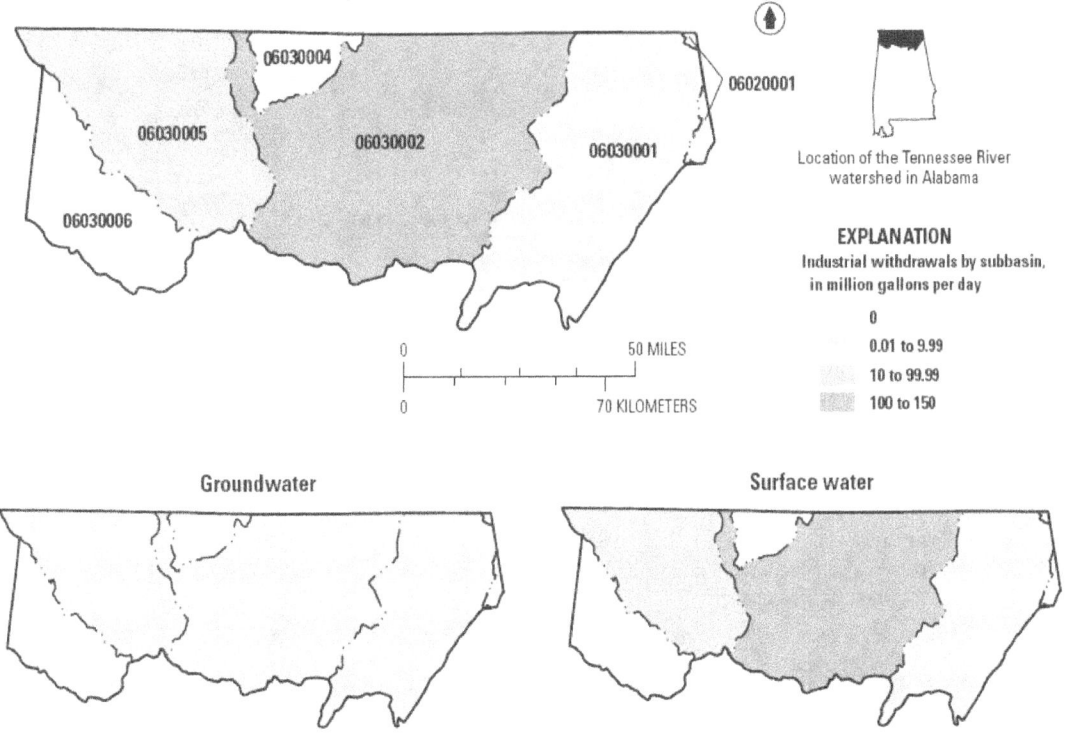

Figure 23.   Self-supplied industrial freshwater withdrawals by source and subbasin in the Tennessee River watershed in Alabama, 2005.

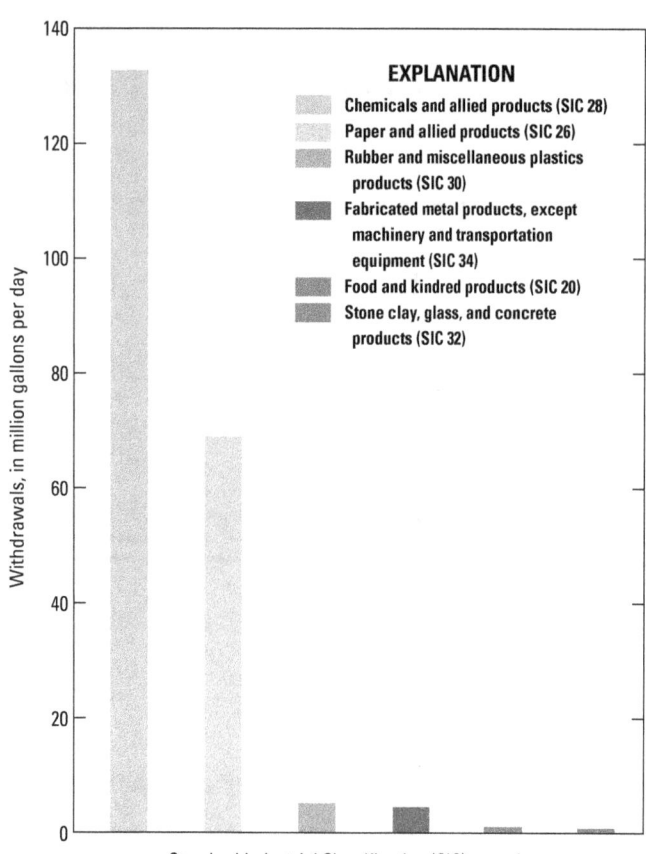

EXPLANATION

- Chemicals and allied products (SIC 28)
- Paper and allied products (SIC 26)
- Rubber and miscellaneous plastics products (SIC 30)
- Fabricated metal products, except machinery and transportation equipment (SIC 34)
- Food and kindred products (SIC 20)
- Stone clay, glass, and concrete products (SIC 32)

Standard Industrial Classification (SIC) grouping

Paper and allied products (Standard Industrial Classification [SIC] 26, 69 Mgal/d) and chemicals and allied products (SIC 28, 133 Mgal/d) accounted for 94 percent of total self-supplied industrial withdrawals in the Tennessee River watershed in Alabama (fig. 24). Chemicals and allied products accounted for the largest self-supplied industrial surface-water withdrawals (133 Mgal/d), and food and kindred products (1 Mgal/d) accounted for the largest self-supplied industrial groundwater withdrawals (table 20).

Figure 24.   Distribution of total industrial withdrawals by Standard Industrial Classification grouping in the Tennessee River watershed within Alabama, 2005.

Table 20.   Self-supplied industrial water withdrawals by Standard Industrial Classification and by source in the Tennessee River watershed in Alabama, 2005.

Standard Industrial Classification		Water withdrawals, in million gallons per day		
		Groundwater	Surface water	Total
20	Food and kindred products	1.18	0.00	1.18
22	Textile mill products	0.00	0.25	0.25
26	Paper and allied products	0.00	69.01	69.01
28	Chemicals and allied products	0.16	132.62	132.78
30	Rubber and miscellaneous plastics products	0.00	5.27	5.27
34	Fabricated metal products, except machinery and transportation equipment	0.87	3.72	4.59
32	Stone, clay, glass, and concrete products	0.00	0.89	0.89
	Total	**2.20**	**211.76**	**213.96**

Mining

Mining water refers to water that is used for the extraction of naturally occurring minerals including solids, such as coal, sand, gravel, and other ores; liquids, such as crude petroleum; and gases, such as natural gas. Mining also includes uses associated with quarrying, milling, and other preparations customarily done at a mine site or as part of a mining activity. Mining water use does not include water associated with dewatering of an aquifer that is not put to beneficial use and also does not include water used in processing, such as smelting, refining petroleum, or slurry pipeline operations. These processing uses are included in the industrial category.

Mining water withdrawals are listed by county in table 21. For the Tennessee River watershed in 2005, total mining withdrawals were 3 Mgal/d, which is less than 0.01 percent of total withdrawals and nearly 0.7 percent of total withdrawals for all categories excluding thermoelectric power (table 5). Groundwater was the source of about 56 percent (1.7 Mgal/d) of withdrawals, and surface water was the source of the remaining 44 percent (1.3 Mgal/d) (fig. 25).

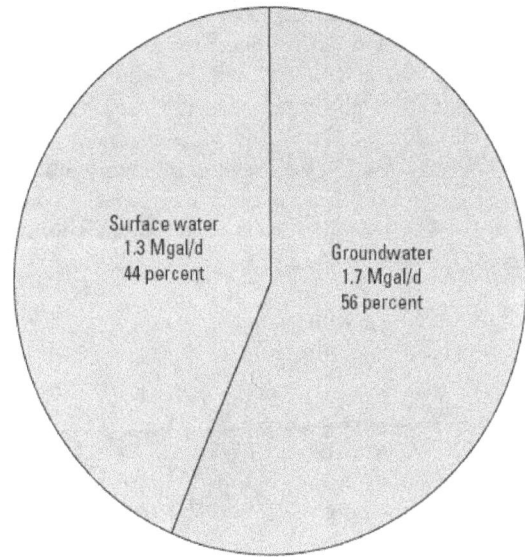

Figure 25. Source of water for mining use in the Tennessee River watershed in Alabama, 2005.

Table 21. Mining water withdrawals, returns, and net demands by county in the Tennessee River watershed within Alabama, 2005.

[Figures may not sum to totals because of independent rounding. County names in **bold** type indicate counties entirely contained within the watershed]

County	Withdrawals, in million gallons per day			Return flow	Consumption, in million gallons per day
	Groundwater	Surface water	Total		Net water demand
Blount	0.04	0.00	0.04	0.00	0.04
Colbert	0.00	0.05	0.05	0.00	0.05
Cullman	0.00	0.00	0.00	0.00	0.00
DeKalb	0.00	0.00	0.00	0.00	0.00
Etowah	0.00	0.00	0.00	0.00	0.00
Franklin	0.39	0.18	0.57	0.00	0.57
Jackson	0.07	0.03	0.10	0.00	0.10
Lauderdale	0.00	0.00	0.00	0.00	0.00
Lawrence	0.16	0.07	0.23	0.00	0.23
Limestone	0.00	0.50	0.50	0.00	0.50
Madison	0.48	0.22	0.70	0.00	0.70
Marion	0.00	0.00	0.00	0.00	0.00
Marshall	0.19	0.09	0.28	0.00	0.28
Morgan	0.37	0.17	0.54	0.00	0.54
Winston	0.00	0.00	0.00	0.00	0.00
Total	**1.70**	**1.31**	**3.01**	**0.00**	**3.01**

The geographic distributions of total, groundwater, and surface-water withdrawals for mining use by county are shown in figure 26. Six of the 15 counties in the Tennessee River watershed had no mining water use in 2005, and each of the counties with mining activities had withdrawals of 0.7 Mgal/d or less (table 21). Most of the permitted mining facilities in the Tennessee River watershed in Alabama were crushed stone or sand and gravel plants. A few coal mines also were operated in this part of Alabama.

Mining water withdrawals were summarized for each of the hydrologic subbasins (table 22; fig. 27). The Middle Tennessee–Chickamauga (HUC 06020001) subbasin in Alabama had no mining activity. The Wheeler Lake (HUC 06030002) subbasin had the greatest mining water withdrawals, 1.39 Mgal/d, or about 46 percent of the mining withdrawals for the Tennessee River watershed in Alabama. Mining water withdrawals in the remaining four subbasins ranged from 0.26 to 0.51 Mgal/d.

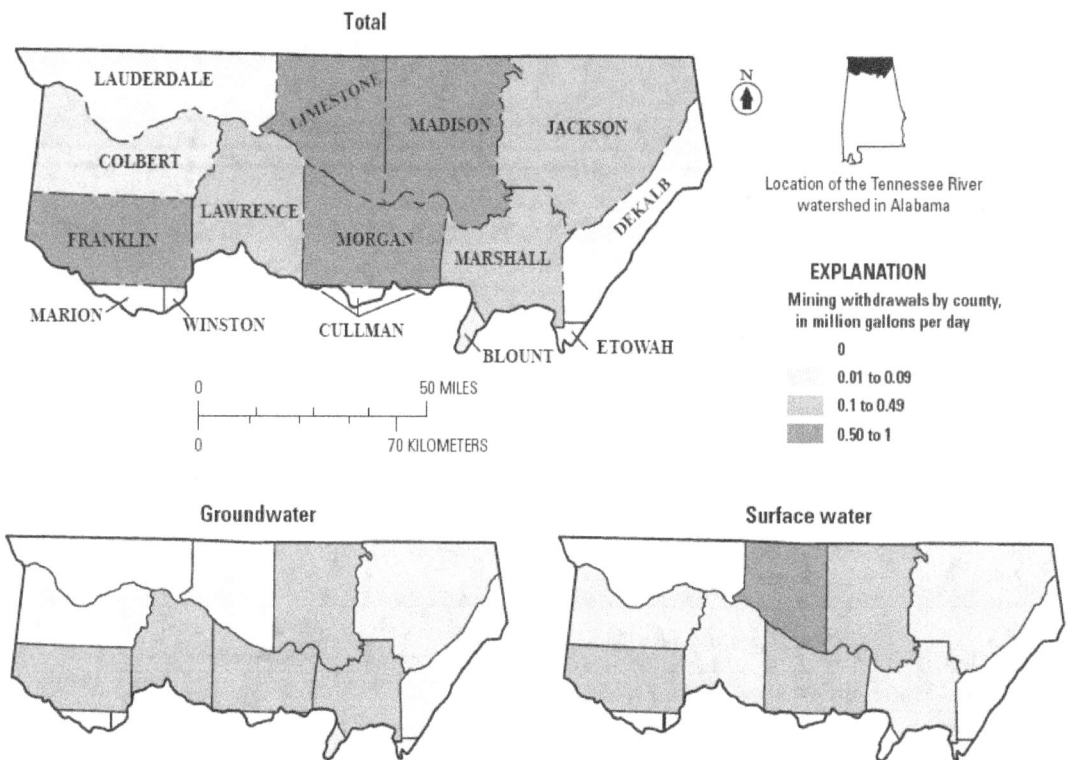

Figure 26.   Mining freshwater withdrawals by source and county in the Tennessee River watershed in Alabama, 2005.

Table 22. Mining water withdrawals, returns, and net demands by hydrologic subregion and subbasin in the Tennessee River watershed within Alabama, 2005.

[Figures may not sum to totals because of independent rounding]

Hydrologic subregion and subbasin		Withdrawals, in million gallons per day			Return flow, in million gallons per day	Consumption, in million gallons per day
		Groundwater	Surface water	Total		Net water demand
Middle Tennessee–Hiwassee						
06020001	Middle Tennessee–Chickamauga	0.00	0.00	0.00	0.00	0.00
Subtotal		0.00	0.00	0.00	0.00	0.00
Middle Tennessee–Elk						
06030001	Guntersville Lake	0.26	0.1	0.36	0.00	0.36
06030002	Wheeler Lake	0.95	0.44	1.39	0.00	1.39
06030004	Lower Elk	0.00	0.5	0.50	0.00	0.50
06030005	Pickwick Lake	0.15	0.11	0.26	0.00	0.26
06030006	Bear	0.34	0.17	0.51	0.00	0.51
Subtotal		1.70	1.32	3.02	0.00	3.02
Total		**1.70**	**1.32**	**3.02**	**0.00**	**3.02**

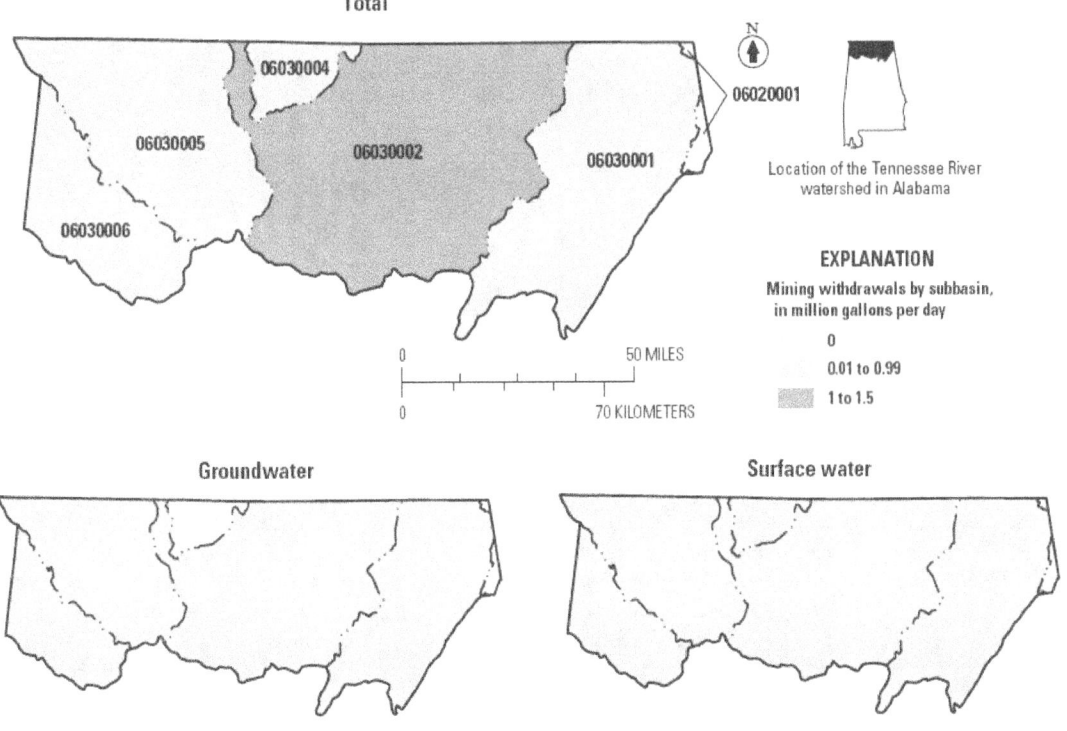

Figure 27. Mining withdrawals by source and subbasin in the Tennessee River watershed in Alabama, 2005.

Thermoelectric Power

Thermoelectric power water is water used in the process of generating electricity with steam-driven turbine generators and for other onsite needs. Once-through cooling (also known as open-loop cooling) of power generation plants refers to cooling systems in which water is withdrawn from a source, circulated through heat exchangers, and then returned to a surface-water body. All thermoelectric-power water use in the Tennessee River watershed in Alabama was for once-through cooling using surface water as the source of cooling water, with more than 99 percent of the cooling water being returned to its source in 2005.

In 2005, four thermoelectric power plants in the Tennessee River watershed in Alabama used 4,762 Mgal/d of surface water for cooling to produce 36,747 gigawatt-hours of energy. Total thermoelectric power water withdrawals are listed by county and hydrologic subbasin in tables 23 and 24. Only four counties in the Tennessee River watershed in Alabama—Colbert (1,294 Mgal/d), Jackson (1,476 Mgal/d), Limestone (1,990 Mgal/d), and Morgan (1 Mgal/d)—had thermoelectric power water withdrawals. These withdrawals occurred in the Guntersville Lake (HUC 06030001; 1,476 Mgal/d), Wheeler Lake (HUC 06030002; 1,991 Mgal/d), and Pickwick Lake (HUC 06030005; 1,294 Mgal/d) subbasins. Thermoelectric power withdrawals accounted for 92 percent of total water withdrawals and 93 percent of total surface-water withdrawals in the Tennessee River watershed in Alabama (tables 5 and 7). The geographic distributions of total withdrawals for thermoelectric power by county and hydrologic subbasin are shown in figures 28 and 29, respectively.

Table 23.   Thermoelectric-power surface-water withdrawals and consumption by county in the Tennessee River watershed within Alabama, 2005.

[Values may not sum to total estimated use(s) because of rounding. County names in **bold** type indicate counties entirely contained within the watershed]

County	Surface-water withdrawals, in million gallons per day	Return flow, in million gallons per day	Consumption, in million gallons per day / Net water demand	Total power generated, in gigawatt-hours
Colbert	1,294.14	1,292.83	1.31	7,743
Jackson	1,476.30	1,476.29	0.01	9,835
Limestone	1,990.24	1,987.54	2.70	17,955
Morgan	1.20	0.40	0.80	1,214
Total	**4,761.88**	**4,757.06**	**4.82**	**36,747**

Table 24.   Thermoelectric-power surface-water withdrawals and consumption, and power generated by hydrologic subregion and subbasin in the Tennessee River watershed within Alabama, 2005.

Hydrologic subregion and subbasin		Surface-water withdrawals, in million gallons per day	Return flow, in million gallons per day	Consumption, in million gallons per day / Net water demand	Total power generated, in gigawatt-hours
		Middle Tennessee–Hiwassee			
06020001	Middle Tennessee–Chickamauga	0.00	0.00	0.00	0
Subtotal		*0.00*	*0.00*	*0.00*	*0*
		Middle Tennessee–Elk			
06030001	Guntersville Lake	1,476.30	1,476.29	0.01	9,835
06030002	Wheeler Lake	1,991.44	1,987.94	3.50	19,169
06030004	Lower Elk	0.00	0.00	0.00	0
06030005	Pickwick Lake	1,294.14	1,292.83	1.31	7,743
06030006	Bear	0.00	0.00	0.00	0
Subtotal		*4,761.88*	*4,757.06*	*4.82*	*36,747*
Total		**4,761.88**	**4,757.06**	**4.82**	**36,747**

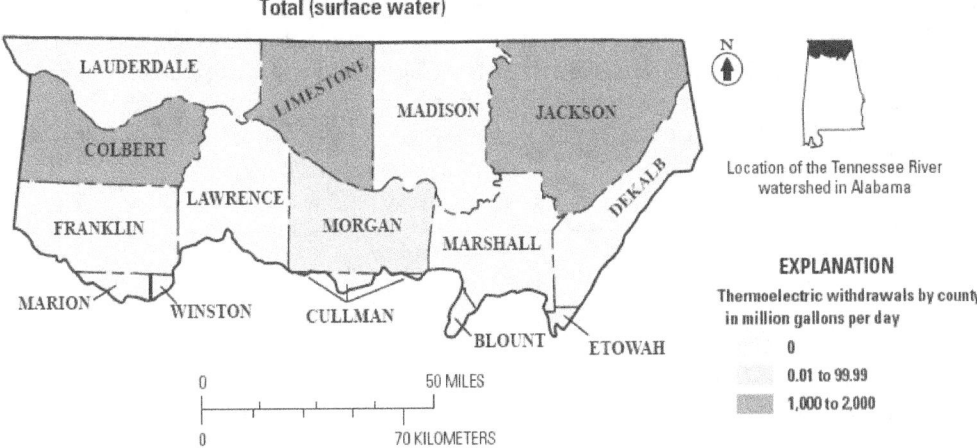

Figure 28. Thermoelectric-power freshwater withdrawals (all surface water) by county in the Tennessee River watershed in Alabama, 2005

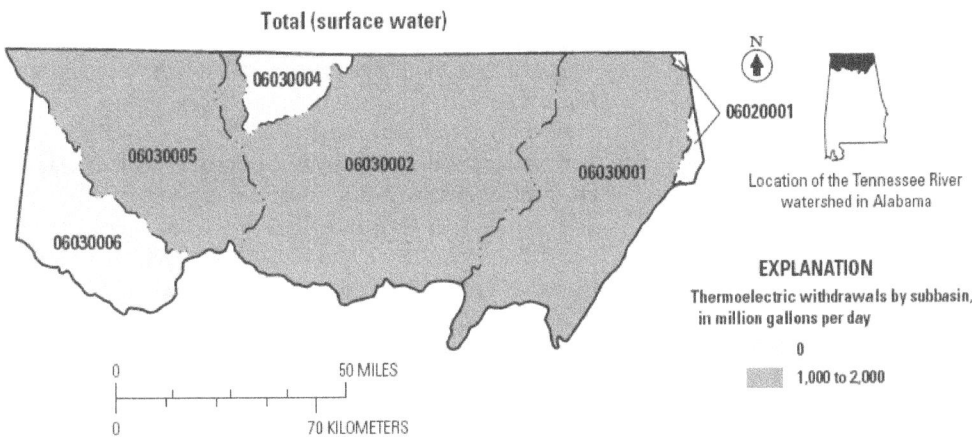

Figure 29. Thermoelectric-power freshwater withdrawals (all surface water) by subbasin in the Tennessee River watershed in Alabama, 2005

Water Availability

Water availability in the Tennessee River watershed of Alabama has previously been described in multiple reports. Most recently, reports by staff of the TVA and the GSA have included estimates of water availability for the region (Bohac and Koroa, 2004; Bohac and McCall, 2008; Cook and others, 2009). The conclusions of these reports are summarized herein to provide an estimate of the water availability in the region.

The GSA estimated amounts of water available to users in the Tennessee River watershed in Alabama from stream-flow data from 20 long-term streamgaging stations. Data from the streamgaging stations were used to estimate groundwater recharge and surface-water availability per unit area (Cook and others, 2009). The methods and results of this investigation are described in further detail in the Groundwater Availability section of this report.

The TVA also assessed surface-water availability and summarized 2005 net water demand for four major water uses in the watershed, compared use in 2005 to previous years, and projected water use for the year 2030 (Bohac and Koroa, 2004; Bohac and McCall, 2008). Withdrawal and return information for 2005 for thermoelectric, public-supply, industrial, and irrigation water uses was summarized by political and hydrologic boundaries.

Groundwater Availability

The amount of available groundwater is related to the amount of storage in the groundwater system. Many of the water-bearing geologic formations in the Tennessee River watershed within Alabama are characterized by fractures and cavities that may provide large amounts of groundwater but are not uniformly distributed (Cook and others, 2009). Though estimates of groundwater availability have been generated for the region, accessibility and availability at any given location in the watershed are largely unknown.

Estimates of baseflow were assumed by Cook and others (2009) to be a reasonable estimate of annual groundwater recharge. In turn, annual groundwater recharge was assumed to be an acceptable estimate of groundwater availability for a given area. Because areas of similar geology and stratigraphy might reasonably be expected to have similar groundwater yield, the GSA designated six geologic areas (fig. 30) of similar characteristics for estimating groundwater availability in the region. The GSA used the recharge rates estimated from the baseflow analyses multiplied by the area of each geologic area to determine a total annual groundwater yield for the geologic area and a rate of recharge/availability in thousand gallons per day per square mile for each geologic area. Based on geologic areas, total groundwater availability for the entire Tennessee River watershed in Alabama was estimated to be 1,967 Mgal/d (Cook and others, 2009; table 25).

Table 25. Estimated available groundwater in the Tennessee River watershed in Alabama (modified from Cook and others, 2009; refer to figure 30 for location of geologic areas).

Geologic area	Available groundwater		
	Billion gallons per year	Million gallons per day	Thousand gallons per day per square mile
1	108.9	298.4	265.2
2	53.8	147.3	158.0
3	304.0	832.8	376.2
4	129.7	355.4	266.6
5	36.2	99.3	262.0
6	85.5	234.1	266.6
Total	**718.1**	**1,967.3**	

Surface-Water Availability

The GSA also estimated surface-water availability for the Tennessee Valley watershed in Alabama (Cook and others, 2009). For the surface-water analysis, the GSA used streamflow data from the same 20 sites used for estimation of groundwater availability. For each site, the mean annual period of record streamflow was divided by the drainage area of the site's watershed. The resulting discharges per unit area, expressed as cubic feet per second per square mile (ft^3/mi^2), were averaged for all sites within a hydrologic unit, and the average unit discharge was used to estimate surface-water availability for the entire area of the hydrologic unit. Average unit discharges and hydrologic-unit surface-water availabilities are summarized in table 26. Total surface-water availability originating in the Tennessee River watershed within Alabama was 8,200 Mgal/d. An additional 24,400 Mgal/d are supplied from the portion of the Tennessee River flowing into Alabama (Cook and others, 2009), so total surface-water availability was estimated to be 32,600 Mgal/d (Cook and others, 2009).

Table 26. Estimated available surface water in the Tennessee River watershed in Alabama (modified from Cook and others, 2009).

[ft^3/mi^2, cubic feet per second per square mile; ft^3/d, cubic feet per day; Mgal/d, million gallons per day]

Hydrologic subbasin	Unit discharge ft^3/mi^2	Available surface water	
		million ft^3/d	Mgal/d
06020001	1.96	8.3	100
06030001	1.96	282.1	2,100
06030002	1.76	403.9	3,000
06030004	1.68	38.2	300
06030005	1.83	225.2	1,700
06030006	1.89	127.2	1,000
Total		**1,084.9**	**8,200**

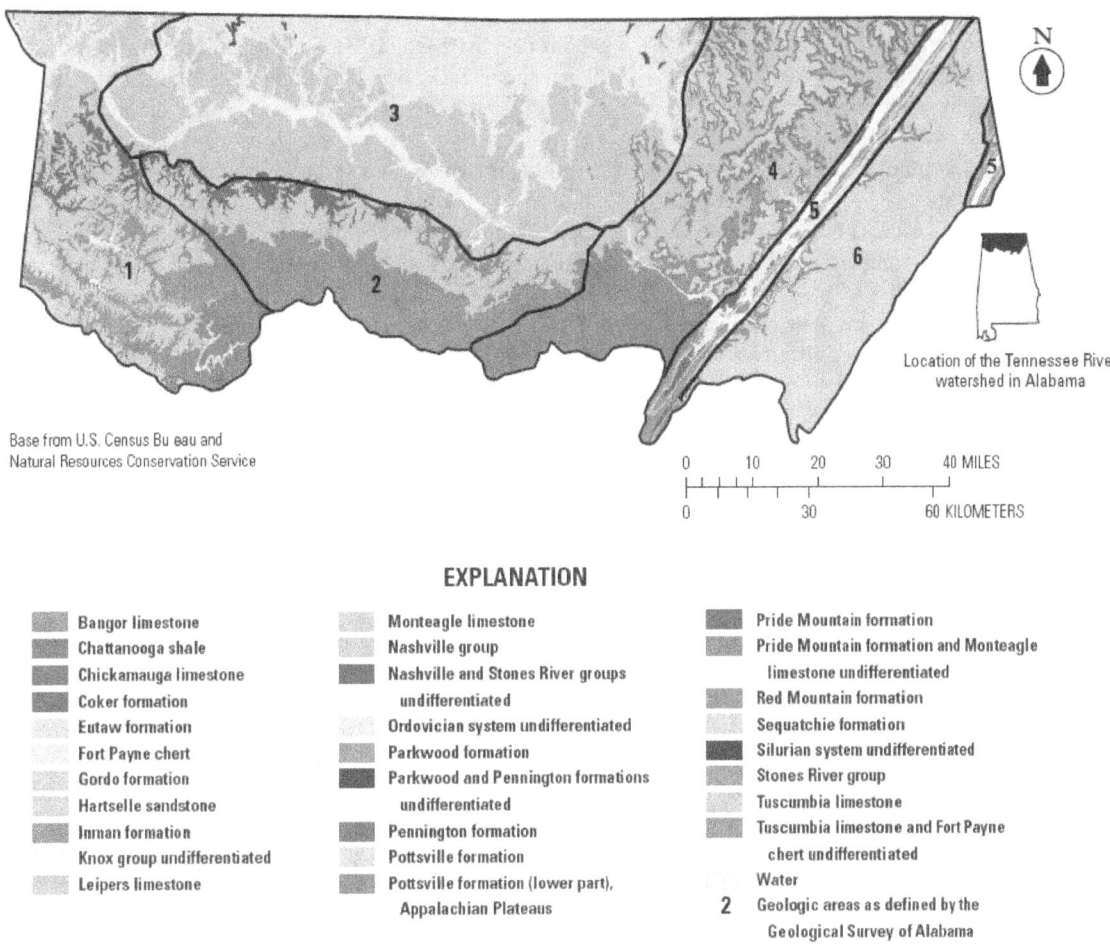

EXPLANATION

Bangor limestone	Monteagle limestone
Chattanooga shale	Nashville group
Chickamauga limestone	Nashville and Stones River groups
Coker formation	undifferentiated
Eutaw formation	Ordovician system undifferentiated
Fort Payne chert	Parkwood formation
Gordo formation	Parkwood and Pennington formations
Hartselle sandstone	undifferentiated
Inman formation	Pennington formation
Knox group undifferentiated	Pottsville formation
Leipers limestone	Pottsville formation (lower part),
	Appalachian Plateaus

Pride Mountain formation
Pride Mountain formation and Monteagle
limestone undifferentiated
Red Mountain formation
Sequatchie formation
Silurian system undifferentiated
Stones River group
Tuscumbia limestone
Tuscumbia limestone and Fort Payne
chert undifferentiated
Water
2   Geologic areas as defined by the
Geological Survey of Alabama

Figure 30.   Geology and geologic areas within the Tennessee River watershed in Alabama. (Modified from Cook and others, 2009.)

Water Availability and Net Water Demand

The GSA estimated availability of approximately 1.967 Mgal/d of groundwater and 8,200 Mgal/d of surface water from the Tennessee River watershed within the State of Alabama. The GSA added the inflow of the Tennessee River to Alabama at an average rate of 24,400 Mgal/d to calculate a total surface-water availability in the Tennessee River watershed in Alabama of 32,600 Mgal/d. Total water availability for the Tennessee River watershed in Alabama including groundwater, surface water flowing into the State, and surface water originating within the State was estimated to be 34,567 Mgal/d.

The TVA evaluated water availability in terms of 2005 use and return flows (Bohac and Koroa, 2004; Bohac and McCall, 2008). The TVA reported water-use amounts similar to those reported by the USGS in this report. Total return

flows for the Tennessee River watershed in Alabama were about 97 percent of total water withdrawn. Approximately 55 percent of public-supply water was returned to the environment through wastewater discharges in the Tennessee River watershed. About 96 percent of the water withdrawn by industrial water users was return flow. Thermoelectric water use in the Tennessee River watershed in Alabama was entirely used for once-through cooling, and almost 100 percent was returned to the environment.

Consumptive water use is the part of the water withdrawn that is evaporated, transpired, incorporated into crops, consumed by humans or livestock, or otherwise is removed from the immediate water environment (Hutson and others, 2009). In this report, consumptive use is referred to as net water demand and is determined from water withdrawal and return flow data at the county and subbasin levels for public supply, self-supplied industrial, and thermoelectric power (Hutson and others, 2004b). Total net water demand for the Tennessee River watershed in Alabama was about 136 Mgal/d (table 3). The total net demands by hydrologic unit (table 4) are lower than the county estimates of net water demand because they do not include residential water withdrawals. Net demands by category in order from largest to smallest were public supply (82 Mgal/d; table 11), irrigation (22 Mgal/d; table 14), industrial (9 Mgal/d; table 18), livestock (7 Mgal/d; table 16), thermoelectric (5 Mgal/d; table 22), and mining (3 Mgal/d; table 20).

According to these summary data, the Tennessee River watershed in Alabama has large amounts of water available for multiple uses. Net demand for consumptive uses totaled less than 1 percent of total water available in 2005. Groundwater is not uniformly distributed across the watershed because of variations in geology and the dimensions of water-bearing rock units, and surface water is geographically limited to streams. Consequently, as noted by the USGS and GSA, not all of the existing water may be easily accessible for consumptive uses. In addition, demand requirements for navigation, recreation, ecological needs, and other uses may compete with increased consumptive uses in the watershed. As water managers plan for future water demands, additional data are needed about (1) the extent and accessibility of groundwater available for withdrawal, (2) the amount of return flows for categories such as self-supplied residential, livestock, and irrigation, and (3) projections of future population and industrial growth.

Summary

Water use, availability, and net water demand data for 2005 were summarized by the U.S. Geological Survey, in cooperation with the Alabama Department of Economic and Community Affairs, Office of Water Resources, for the Alabama portion of the Tennessee River watershed. State managers have identified the Tennessee River watershed within Alabama as a high-priority area for future water use planning for the State of Alabama because the watershed has high water withdrawal rates, some of the Alabama's large population centers, thermoelectric power generation, and industry, and a Federal interest in the flow of the river.

Total water use for the study area was 5,197 million gallons per day (Mgal/d). Surface water accounted for 99 percent, or 5,139 Mgal/d, of the water used, while only about 58 Mgal/d of groundwater was used in the study area.

Water use was summarized by categories of water use and by county and 8-digit hydrologic subbasin. County-level estimates of water use were made for public-supply, self-supplied residential, industrial, mining, livestock, irrigation, and thermoelectric water use categories. Hydrologic unit estimates of water use were made for all of the same categories except self-supplied residential. The greatest uses of water in the region were thermoelectric power generation (4,762 million gallons per day [Mgal/d], 92 percent of total use), followed by self-supplied industrial (214 Mgal/d, 4 percent of total use) and public supply (181 Mgal/d, 4 percent of total use). The counties and subbasins where thermoelectric power generation takes place (Limestone, Jackson, and Colbert Counties; subbasins 06030001, 06030002, and 06030005) had the greatest withdrawals and use. When thermoelectric power generation was not considered, Morgan, Madison, Colbert, and Lawrence Counties and subbasin 06030002 had the greatest withdrawals.

Water availability estimates and information compiled by the Geological Survey of Alabama (GSA) and the Tennessee Valley Authority (TVA) were summarized. The GSA estimated that the total water availability in the Tennessee River watershed within Alabama is 34,567 Mgal/d (1,967 Mgal/d of groundwater, 8,200 Mgal/d of surface water from the Tennessee River watershed within the State of Alabama, and 24,400 Mgal/d inflow of the Tennessee River to Alabama). The TVA reported that about 97 percent of total water withdrawn was returned to the environment, and the resulting net demand (136 Mgal/d) accounted for less than 1 percent of estimated available water. These data indicate that the Tennessee River watershed in Alabama has large amounts of water available for multiple uses. As noted by the USGS and GSA, however, not all of the existing water may be easily accessible. Additional data are needed about (1) the extent and accessibility of groundwater available for withdrawal, (2) the amount of return flows for water-use categories such as self-supplied residential, livestock, and irrigation, and (3) projections of future population and industrial growth, to improve future water demand estimations and regional water-use planning.

References

Alabama Department of Conservation and Natural Resources, 2008, Tennessee River—Fish and fishing in the Alabama portion of the Tennessee River, accessed November 1, 2011, at *http://www.dcnr.state.al.us/fishing/freshwater/where/rivers/tennessee/*.

Alabama Development Office, 2004, Alabama industrial directory, 2003–2004: Montgomery, Alabama, 557 p.

Baker, R.M., 1989, Water availability in Jackson County, Alabama: Geological Survey of Alabama Special Map 209, 84 p., 2 pls.

Baker, R.M., and Moser, P.H., 1989, Water availability in DeKalb County, Alabama: Geological Survey of Alabama Special Map 215, 71 p., 2 pls.

Bohac, C.E., and Koroa, M.C., 2004, Tennessee Valley water supply inventory and needs analysis: Tennessee Valley Authority [variously paged].

Bohac, C.E., and McCall, M.J., 2008, Water use in the Tennessee Valley for 2005 and projected use in 2030: Tennessee Valley Authority [variously paged].

Bossong, C.R., 1989, Geohydrology and susceptibility of major aquifers to surface contamination in Alabama; Area 2: U.S. Geological Survey Water-Resources Investigations Report 88–4177, 22 p.

Bossong, C.R., and Harris, W.F., 1987, Geohydrology and susceptibility of major aquifers to surface contamination in Alabama; Area 1: U.S. Geological Survey Water-Resources Investigations Report 87–4068, 34 p.

Cook, M.R., Moss, N.E., and Jennings, S.P., 2009, Ground-water hydrogeology, recharge, and water availability in the Tennessee River watershed of Alabama: Geological Survey of Alabama Open-File Report 0910, 44 p.

Energy Information Administration, 2008, EIA–767 data files, annual steam-electric plant operation and design data, accessed November 6, 2008, at *http://www.eia.doe.gov/cneaf/electricity/page/eia767.html*.

Energy Information Administration, 2009a, Form EIA–906 and EIA-920 databases, accessed January 27, 2009, at *http://www.eia.doe.gov/cneaf/electricity/page/eia906_920.html*.

Energy Information Administration, 2009b, Electric power annual 2007—Data tables, accessed January 27, 2009, at *http://www.eia.doe.gov/cneaf/electricity/epa/epa_sprdshts.html*.

Hunter, J.A., 1991, Ground water availability in Limestone County, Alabama: Geological Survey of Alabama Special Map 226, 60 p., 2 pls.

Hutson, S.S., Barber, N.L., Kenny, J.F., Linsey, K.S., Lumia, D.S., and Maupin, M.A., 2004a, Estimated use of water in the United States in 2000: U.S. Geological Survey Circular 1268, 46 p.

Hutson, S.S., Koroa, M.C., and Murphree, C.M., 2004b, Estimated use of water in the Tennessee River watershed in 2000 and projections of water use to 2030: U.S. Geological Survey Water-Resources Investigations Report 03–4302, 89 p.

Hutson, S.S., Littlepage, T.M., Harper, M.J., and Tinney J.O., 2009, Estimated use of water in Alabama in 2005: U.S. Geological Survey Scientific Investigations Report 2009–5163, 210 p.

Kammerer, J.C., 1976, Water quantity requirements for public supplies and other uses, in Gehm, H.W., and Bregman, J.I., Handbook of water resources and pollution control: New York, N.Y., Van Nostrand Reinhold Co., p. 44–83.

MacKichan, K.A., 1951, Estimated water use in the United States, 1950: U.S. Geological Survey Circular 115, 13 p.

MacKichan, K.A., 1957, Estimated water use in the United States, 1955: U.S. Geological Survey Circular 398, 18 p.

MacKichan, K.A., and Kammerer, J.C., 1961, Estimated water use in the United States, 1960: U.S. Geological Survey Circular 456, 26 p.

Miller, J.A., 1990, Groundwater atlas of the United States—Alabama, Florida, Georgia, and South Carolina: U.S. Geological Survey Hydrologic Atlas 730-G, accessed October 5, 2012, at *http://pubs.usgs.gov/ha/ha730/ch_g/index.html*.

Mooty, W.S., and Richardson, J.R., 1998, Water use in Alabama, 1995: U.S. Geological Survey Water-Resources Investigations Report 98–4154, 92 p.

Murray, C.R., 1968, Estimated water use in the United States, 1965: U.S. Geological Survey Circular 556, 53 p.

Murray, C.R., and Reeves, E.B., 1972, Estimated water use in the United States, 1970: U.S. Geological Survey Circular 676, 37 p.

Murray, C.R., and Reeves, E.B., 1977, Estimated water use in the United States, 1975: U.S. Geological Survey Circular 765, 37 p.

National Oceanic and Atmospheric Administration, 2009, Monthly station normals, accessed January 5, 2011, at *http://cdo.ncdc.noaa.gov/cgi-bin/climatenormals/climatenormals.pl*.

Solley, W.B., Chase, E.B., and Mann, W.B., IV, 1983, Estimated water use in the United States, 1980: U.S. Geological Survey Circular 1001, 56 p.

Solley, W.B., Merk, C.F., and Pierce, R.R., 1988, Estimated water use in the United States, 1985: U.S. Geological Survey Circular 1004, 82 p.

Solley, W.B., Pierce, R.R., and Perlman, H.A., 1993, Estimated water use in the United States, 1990: U.S. Geological Survey Circular 1081, 71 p.

Solley, W.B., Pierce, R.R., and Perlman, H.A., 1998, Estimated use of water in the United States in 1995: U.S. Geological Survey Circular 1200, 71 p.

Tennessee Valley Authority, 2012, River management, accessed October 9, 2012, at *http://www.tva.com/river/index.htm.*

TheGolfCourses.net, 2009, Golf courses in Alabama, accessed January 4, 2013, at *http://www.thegolfcourses.net/golf-courses/AL/Alabama.htm.*

The University of Alabama, Center for Business and Economic Research, 2011, Alabama county population 2000–2010 and projections 2015–2035 (Interim Series), accessed June 21, 2012, at *http://cber.cba.ua.edu/edata/est_prj.html.*

U.S. Census Bureau, 1992, 1990 Census of population and housing, summary of social, economic, and housing characteristics—Alabama: Washington, D.C., U.S. Department of Commerce report 1990 CPH–5–2, 218 p., Appendixes A–F, accessed September 12, 2007, at *http://www.census.gov/prod/cen1990/cph5/cph-5-2.pdf.*

U.S. Census Bureau, 2006a, Annual estimates of the population for counties, April 1, 2000 to July 1, 2005 (Alabama), accessed March 21, 2006, at *http://www.census.gov/popest/counties/CO-EST2005-01.html.*

U.S. Census Bureau, 2006b, Cumulative estimates of population change for counties of Alabama and county rankings, April 1, 2000 to July 1, 2005, accessed September 23, 2010, at *http://www.census.gov/popest/counties/CO-EST2005-02.html.*

U.S. Census Bureau, Geography Division, 2001, Census 2000 TIGER/Line® Files, accessed September 21, 2010, at *http://www.census.gov/geo/www/tiger/tiger2k/tgr2000.html.*

U.S. Department of Agriculture, 2004, Federal standards for delineation of hydrologic unit boundaries, version 2.0, October 1, 2004, accessed September 15, 2008, at *ftp://ftp-fc.sc.egov.usda.gov/NCGC/products/watershed/hu-standards.pdf.*

U.S. Department of Agriculture, Soil Conservation Service, 1993, State of Alabama hydrologic unit map with drainage areas by counties and sub-watershed, Appendixes A–F.

U.S. Department of Agriculture, National Agricultural Statistics Service, 2004a, 2002 Census of agriculture, Alabama, state and county data—Volume 1, Geographic area series, Part 1, AC–02–A–1, accessed September 12, 2007, at *http://www.agcensus.usda.gov/Publications/2002/Volume_1,_Chapter_1_State_Level/Alabama/index.asp.*

U.S. Department of Agriculture, National Agricultural Statistics Service, 2004b, 2002 Census of agriculture, 2003 farm and ranch irrigation survey—Volume 3, Special studies, Part 1, AC–02–SS–1, 176 p., accessed September 12, 2007, at *http://www.agcensus.usda.gov/Publications/2002/FRIS/index.asp.*

U.S. Department of Agriculture, National Agricultural Statistics Service, 2006a, Alabama Agricultural Statistics: Bulletin 48, 96 p.

U.S. Department of Agriculture, National Agricultural Statistics Service, 2006b, U.S. poultry—Production and value, 2005 summary, 10 p.

U.S. Environmental Protection Agency, 2009, Safe drinking water query form for the State of Alabama, accessed January 27, 2009, at *http://oaspub.epa.gov/enviro/sdw_form_v2.create_page?state_abbr=AL/.*

U.S. Geological Survey, 2007a, Facing tomorrow's challenges—U.S. Geological Survey science in the decade 2007–2017: U.S. Geological Survey Circular 1309, 67 p.

U.S. Geological Survey, 2007b, Boundary descriptions and names of regions, subregions, accounting units and cataloging units (Region 03), accessed November 26, 2008, at *http://water.usgs.gov/GIS/huc_name.html#Region03.*

U.S. Geological Survey, 2012, WaterWatch, accessed September 25, 2012, at *http://waterwatch.usgs.gov.*